Thy Will
Be Done?

Thy Will
Be Done?

Trusting God in the Midst of Suffering, Pain, or Loss

Gabriel O'Sullivan

WinePressPublishing
Great Books, Defined.

WinePress Publishing (PO Box 428, Enumclaw, WA 98022) functions only as book publisher. As such, the ultimate design, content, editorial accuracy, and views expressed or implied in this work are those of the author.

Unless otherwise noted, all Scriptures are taken from the *Holy Bible, New International Version®, NIV®*. Copyright © 1973, 1978, 1984 by Biblica, Inc.™ Used by permission of Zondervan. All rights reserved worldwide. www.zondervan.com

ISBN 13: 978-1-4141-2298-4
ISBN 10: 1-4141-2298-5
Library of Congress Catalog Card Number: 2012901471

Contents

Prologue

SOMETIMES LIFE THROWS curveballs that hit us in the face. Sometimes life sneaks up on us and hits us in the back of the head with a baseball bat. We know where we stand with the curveball. We're in the batter's box, and the pitch is coming. It may not be what we expect, but we are prepared to take the pitch. Not so with the bat to the back of the head. We're totally oblivious. Before we know it, *Wham!* That's all she wrote.

The question is, What will we do next? Will we stand in for another pitch and swing for the fences? Will we pick ourselves up from the ground, wipe off the blood, and continue forward? Or will we just lie there and give up? We all face this kind of decision sooner or later in life; many of us will confront it numerous times.

How do we see the circumstances when our faces catch the curveballs or the back of our heads catch the bats? Do we see things as part of God's amazing and glorious plan? Or do we see them as God's punishment? Are they testimonies of God's wonderful ability to bring himself glory, or will they lead us in the direction of abandoning our faith?

I pray this book will draw you nearer to the loving arms of your all-powerful, all-knowing, and completely in-control Creator. He loves you no matter what life may be telling you right now.

Chapter 1

The Beginning

I have told you these things, so that in me you may
have peace. In this world you will have trouble. But
take heart! I have overcome the world.
—John 16:33

I RUSHED OUT of my office trying not to sound panicked
as I told my receptionist I was leaving a little early for
lunch. My wife, Ryanne, was not feeling well and I needed
to check on her. She was twenty-four weeks pregnant with
our triplet girls. I had talked to her a minute before and
was alarmed to learn she was at her OB's office because the
pressure she had been experiencing the previous night in
her lower abdomen had returned and intensified as that
Friday morning wore on. She was scheduled to go on an
overnight trip with some ladies from church and wanted to
get examined just in case something was not right. Although
Ryanne seemed so calm and told me not to worry, I started
speeding toward her doctor's office.

Ryanne had stopped working four weeks before, and now she was on bed rest. Working was not an option any longer for such a small-framed girl pregnant with triplets. It was too hard to sit at her computer and too much stress managing our busy chiropractic clinic.

A few minutes into my commute, Ryanne called. She was sobbing and told me to pick her up at the OB's office immediately. She was dilated to 4 cm, in preterm labor, and needed to be admitted to the hospital. I instantly prayed, "Please, God, reverse this!" I believed with all my heart that he would. God answers the prayers of his faithful, and I considered myself faithful.

I bolted into her doctor's office, and the receptionist took me straight to Ryanne's room. She was lying down in a recliner and began crying as soon as I walked in. "I am so sorry," she started.

"Sorry for what?" I asked. "You've done nothing wrong."

As we helped Ryanne into a wheelchair, her nurse explained the situation. Ryanne's cervix had thinned and begun dilating. This happens sometimes with single-baby pregnancies, but it is much more common with multiple births. The nurse assured us it was not anything we had done wrong, but that these things happen sometimes for no apparent reason and with no warning. Ryanne had followed all the advice given to her by the high-risk OB she consulted on her triplet pregnancy. She had been drinking plenty of water, lying down for two hours, three times a day, and had been staying off her feet for long periods of time. She had done everything right.

"How could this have happened?" we wondered. More pointedly, "How could God have allowed this to happen?"

Ryanne's condition occurred all of a sudden. We had just been to see the doctor a few days prior. She'd had an ultrasound that day, and the ultrasound nurse could not see the width of Ryanne's cervix. She said it was surely intact because my wife was showing no signs of pre-term labor and the babies were all doing great. I now wonder if the cervical lining was actually intact that day, and I wish I would have insisted the nurse be more persistent. But I didn't.

The nurse continued to reassure us that Ryanne had not done anything wrong. I had serious guilt feelings for asking Ryanne to meet me for dinner the night before after she had told me she was feeling uncomfortable pressure down in her abdomen. Why didn't I tell her to go home, lie down, and put her feet up? Why didn't I take her to the hospital then? I felt so bad for taking no action. I had obstetrics classes in college. How did I miss this?

The nurse helped me get Ryanne into the car and told us to recline her seat on our way to the hospital. This would take a lot of pressure off her cervix. It was obvious Ryanne could go into full labor at any second, so I wondered why we were not being transported to the hospital in an ambulance. Once she was situated in the car, we raced away to the hospital. Ryanne was sobbing, and I was in a panic.

Chapter 2

When God's Plan Involves Our Suffering, Can We Trust It?

DEATH, WAR, 9/11, famine, plague, divorce, bankruptcy, adultery, natural disasters, homelessness, job loss, suicide. These and other tragic circumstances or events cause us to wonder if there is a God. If there is, why would he allow us to suffer if he really loves us? Can we ever trust a God who allows such misery, pain, heartache, and tragedy to befall us?

We hear "God is Love." How do we square this with the unloving reality of our awful circumstance? Does it make sense that a God who is big enough to create the universe can't heal our loved one or save our marriage? It is not hard to understand that in the midst of a terrible situation many ask why God allowed something to happen to them. They ask, "Why didn't God answer my prayer?"

We struggle to grasp the concept that maybe—just maybe—the world doesn't revolve around us. We are hurt to the core when we realize for the first time that God is not at our beck and call. We have difficulty piecing together who God is—or *if* he is. We question everything we thought we knew about God. Our entire worldview becomes rearranged. Where can we turn? Can we ever look to him and trust him again? Does he still love us?

Ryanne and I posed our share of these questions as we entered the trials with our little girls. One minute we were riding high as the proud, expectant parents of three beautiful girls; the next minute we were on our way to the hospital, battling preterm labor and facing the possibility of losing our babies. After basking in the glow of God's unlimited favor, we seemed to be thrown into the shadow of a place where God wouldn't even be able to find us. It all seemed so unfair.

Perseverance Glorifies God

Moses surely felt this way when he escaped the hands of the Egyptians and found himself wandering the desert for forty years with an entire nation of ungrateful complainers. He led them to the Promised Land, but he was never able to enter it himself. He had been faithful, or so he thought. What was fair about that?

And what about the disciples of Jesus? They followed him closely. They did all he asked them to do and more, but they suffered intense persecution and most were killed for doing what their Master had instructed them.

Jesus knew they would face what they faced. He knew Ryanne and I would end up at the hospital that Friday night in February. He also knew *you* would go through the difficult and nonsensical situations you have gone through. That is why Jesus said in John 16:33, "I have told you these things, so that in me you may have peace. In this world you will have trouble. But take heart! I have overcome the world." Nothing escapes the God of creation! In his divine plan, which included his own incomprehensible suffering and crucifixion, he knew his followers would experience pain. He also knew we wouldn't fully understand why. We can't grasp why our precious wives go into preterm labor and scare us to death. We can't fathom why our wonderful parents or other family members contract terrible diseases and die. We can't make sense of violence and murder, or reconcile how our business failed after we put so much into it. It is beyond our comprehension when our husband or wife seeks affection outside of marriage. There are so many things in this world that are grossly unfair—and God knew we would see it that way.

It does not surprise God that we do not fully comprehend the situation for what it truly is. He reminds us that "I have told you these things, so that in me you may have peace." We will not find peace in our circumstances, our family, our possessions, our jobs, or anything else. We will only find it in Christ. But how do we find peace in a God who allows such misery? The truth is that we may never fully know. If we search the Scriptures, we can find places where God allowed the suffering of his servants. Very often, the reason for the suffering is never completely explained. An example of this is found in the book of Job:

> One day the angels came to present themselves before the Lord, and Satan also came with them. The Lord said to Satan, "Where have you come from?" Satan answered the Lord, "From roaming throughout the earth, going back and forth on it." Then the Lord said to Satan, "Have you considered my servant Job? There is no one on earth like him; he is blameless and upright, a man who fears God and shuns evil." "Does Job fear God for nothing?" Satan replied. "Have you not put a hedge around him and his household and everything he has? You have blessed the work of his hands, so that his flocks and herds are spread throughout the land. But now stretch out your

hand and strike everything he has, and he will surely curse you to your face." The Lord said to Satan, "Very well, then, everything he has is in your power, but on the man himself do not lay a finger." Then Satan went out from the presence of the Lord. One day when Job's sons and daughters were feasting and drinking wine at the oldest brother's house, a messenger came to Job and said, "The oxen were plowing and the donkeys were grazing nearby, and the Sabeans attacked and made off with them. They put the servants to the sword, and I am the only one who has escaped to tell you!" While he was still speaking, another messenger came and said, "The fire of God fell from the heavens and burned up the sheep and the servants, and I am the only one who has escaped to tell you!" While he was still speaking, another messenger came and said, "The Chaldeans formed three raiding parties and swept down on your camels and made off with them. They put the servants to the sword, and I am the only one who has escaped to tell you!" While he was still speaking, yet another messenger came and said, "Your sons and daughters were feasting and drinking wine at the oldest brother's house, when suddenly a mighty wind swept in from the desert and struck the four corners of the house. It collapsed on them and they are dead, and I am the only one who has escaped to tell you!"

—Job 1:6-19

It seems the only reason Job experienced tragedy was because God wanted to use him and his situation as a game of sorts. God put his servant to the test to prove his point against Satan's opinion of Job's character. It is as if God was using Job as a high-stakes poker chip in a hand against Satan. God allowed all that Job had to be laid out on the table in a wager against the enemy. God tells Satan, "Everything he has is in your power, but on the man himself do not lay a finger" (Job 1:12). However, later in the book we find out God *does* give permission for Satan to "lay a finger" on Job, and he becomes deathly sick. At that point, just about everything has been stripped from Job, including his children, wealth, and good health. All for some sort of crazy, heavenly wager. Why?

Everything God does is ultimately for his glory. Jesus said "I am not seeking glory for myself; but there is one who seeks it, and he is the judge" (John 8:50). As the Lord's children and servants, sometimes we are a part of that process, and sometimes that process is not pleasant. Also, God does not want us to trust in anything except him. We are not to rely on health, prosperity, or even family. Our faith is to be in God alone, who wants all generations to learn from Job. No matter what we go through, if we remain faithful and steadfast in our trust in the ultimate goodness of God, our perseverance will glorify him and allow us to manage life's unmanageable situations.

God Really Does Love Us

God really does love us ... intimately, deeply, and more than we will ever be able to comprehend. Although he loves us and is sovereign over all things, bad things will no doubt happen to us. It is not a perfect world, and God's children are not immune to suffering. Yet, we can trust God because his plans are perfect, even if we find them hard to lay hold of.

I hope you have never known suffering and never will. But if you do, I want to give you the opportunity to work out your feelings, frustrations, questions, and misunderstandings about circumstances you have faced, are facing now, or will face in the future. That is what this book is about. I believe the points I address in these pages will help you make it through to each new day.

9

Reflection Questions

1. What made you want to read this book?
2. What questions do you hope this book will answer?
3. Do you think it is fair that you have suffered as you have? Why or why not?
4. If you could, what would you ask God to do in the middle of a trying circumstance?
5. Would you be all right if you never received and answer to your question? Why or why not?
6. Are you angry at God for not intervening during a painful interlude in your life? Or for intervening in an unexpected way?
7. Write a prayer asking God to help you understand why you have had to go through your tragic circumstance. Ask him to help you accept his will for your life so you can move on to find peace in Christ.

Chapter 3

In the Hands of the Almighty

Where can I go from your Spirit? Where can I flee
from your presence? If I go up to the heavens, you are
there; if I make my bed in the depths, you are there.
—Ps. 139:7-8

A S WE DROVE to the hospital, Ryanne eventually
became calm and collected. I can't say the same for
myself; I was overwhelmed with worry. I prayed silently
for God's supernatural intervention and assured Ryanne
that everything was going to be fine. But I doubted more
than I believed.

We pulled up to the Labor and Delivery parking garage.
There was a gate and a speaker box, like the drive through
at a fast food restaurant. I spoke into the box and told the
nurse my wife was a patient and we had been told to come.
After we parked, we entered the building and made our way
to the L&D nurses' desk on the second floor. The nurses
were not expecting our arrival. They looked at us like we
were crazy. The OB office was supposed to have called

over and informed them of our situation. Apparently, the call had not been made—or these particular nurses were not privy to the emergency. Luckily, Ryanne's doctor sent some papers with us to give to the nurses. As soon as they saw the paperwork, their eyes widened and their attitude dramatically changed.

A great deal of activity ensued as they took us to a triage room. The nurses gave Ryanne a gown and told her to lie down on the bed as soon as she changed. A large cart was brought into the room with a fetal monitoring machine to check that our babies' hearts were still beating. I had heard of preterm labor before, but I had never heard of preterm babies being in danger. I was uninformed and unprepared for this crisis. I should have paid more attention in my OB classes.

The fetal monitoring indicated the girls were okay. Their hearts were beating exceptionally well. The next step was an ultrasound by the neonatologist. The ultrasound showed one of our baby's feet protruding through the opening in Ryanne's dilated cervix. Thankfully, Ryanne's water had not broken. The foot was down, but not out of the womb. The neonatologist explained that if Ryanne's cervix dilated any more and that if the baby's foot protruded more, then her water could break and that would mean immediate delivery. Since she was only twenty-four weeks into the pregnancy, the babies' chances of survival would be slim.

Next, Ryanne had a shot of steroids to help speed the development of the girls' lungs. This involved a huge needle right in her thigh. She squeezed my hand and said it felt like the nurse was injecting her with pudding because the medicine felt so thick and went in so slowly. Ryanne was simultaneously catheterized while she got the injection of steroid. This had to be done because she would not be getting out of bed until the girls were born some eight to ten weeks out. Ryanne couldn't risk putting more pressure on her cervix, so standing, sitting, or getting up to go to the bathroom were now forbidden.

Psychic Anguish

Several nurses continued working on her and doing all sorts of different things. Ryanne's case was unique enough to attract student nurses, who were milled around the room, watching things unfold. That tiny ten-by-twelve-foot room was packed with people, activity, and tension, and Ryanne, in the middle of it all, was the star attraction. She was in agony from the pressure of the labor, the injections, the IVs, and the catheter. There was also intense psychic anguish from the terrifying thought that she could lose her babies. The situation was looking bleaker and bleaker for our girls. Each time I saw them administer a procedure on Ryanne, I almost passed out from the thought of her pain. I felt like a real sissy. She was having all this done to her, and I was the one getting queasy. Thank God we both made it through the madding rush without either one of us getting knocked out cold.

After the commotion, the neonatologist told us that Ryanne was now a permanent resident of the Spartanburg Regional Hospital Labor and Delivery unit until our babies were born. He hoped that would be at least two months, which would still be six to eight weeks earlier than the normal gestation time. He said that if they were born at thirty-two weeks, then they should be fine and have little or no health issues.

Ryanne would have to remain lying down in an inverted position, with the head of her bed lower than her feet during that entire time. He told us that she could switch from left to right, but she could not sit up.

This had happened to one of our friends just a few weeks prior to all this. She was pregnant and in the hospital for seven weeks of preterm observation. She was only carrying one baby, but the pressure on the lower abdomen probably made her just as miserable. Like Ryanne, she had to lie down all the time. Ryanne and I commented about how terrible that would have to be. "Poor girl," we thought. Now it was Ryanne's turn, and our journey was just beginning.

Chapter 4

Who is In Charge?
What is He Like?
What Does He
Want?

I T HAS BEEN my experience that during a time of suffering Scripture is sometimes difficult to grasp and even
more difficult to fully believe. Therefore, we will explore
some passages from the Bible together and see what they
say about God and his nature.

God Is Eternal and the Creator

Isaiah 40:28 reads, "Do you not know? Have you not
heard? The Lord is the everlasting God, the Creator of the
ends of the earth. He will not grow tired or weary, and
his understanding no one can fathom." Notice the word
everlasting. This means that God has never had a beginning,
and he will never have an end. He lives forever, upholding
and governing the totality of the universe, from everlasting
to everlasting. We will never know what the Lord knows.
He never becomes tired or is ever in need of rest.

Our Creator Is in Charge

Psalm 24:1 states that "The earth is the Lord's, and everything in it, the world, and all who live in it." Here, the psalmist sums up who is in charge of our lives and all life everywhere. We do not own the earth, and we do not run it. We have just been placed here by the Lord.

He Is Our King and Lord

Who runs the show? The King of glory. "Who is he, this King of glory? The Lord Almighty—he is the King of glory" (Ps. 24:10). Nothing is clearer from Scripture than that God is the One in charge. He is the Lord, the Creator, and the King of Glory.

He Is the Only God

This King of glory is the One and only. Deuteronomy 6:4 says, "Hear, O Israel, the Lord our God, the Lord is One." He is one, and there are no others. Happy are those who have this one Lord as Master, for, as Matthew Henry once said, it is better to have one fountain than a thousand cisterns; one all-sufficient God than a thousand insufficient friends.

He Is One Holy, Triune God as Father, Son, and Holy Spirit

John 5:26 reads, "For as the Father has life in himself, so he has granted the Son to have life in himself." This verse details God as the Father and the Son, and it states that the Father and Son both have life in the Father. First Corinthians 3:16 asks, "Don't you know that you yourselves are God's temple and that God's Spirit dwells in your midst?" The triune God is three Persons in one divine being called the Godhead.

He Is Just

"The leaders of Israel and the king humbled themselves and said, 'The Lord is just'" (2 Chronicles 12:16). When we humble ourselves like the princes and the king of Israel humbled themselves in 2 Chronicles, we will also find that God is just and will defend us.

He Is Faithful

God is also faithful. "Go, proclaim this message toward the north: 'Return, faithless Israel,' declares the Lord, 'I will frown on you no longer, for I am faithful,' declares the Lord, 'I will not be angry forever'" (Jer. 3:12 NIV).

He Is Holy

"I am the Lord your God; consecrate yourselves and be holy, because I am holy" (Lev. 11:44a). God is separate, set apart, distinct, totally pure, and elevated. God calls us to try and be as He is.

He Is Love

First John 4:16 states, "And so we know and rely on the love God has for us. God is love. Whoever lives in love lives in God, and God in them." God is love personified. Every good and perfect thing that love should be is embodied in the person of God. When we can't understand this statement, we must accept it on faith with the hopes that one day we will be able to grasp it.

17

These are just some of the attributes of the loving, perfect, holy God. Since he is above all, the list of God's characteristics would certainly be limitless. We could not describe them all if we tried, but this list is a good start in answering the question of who is in charge and what he is like. What does he want from us?

He Wants Us to Do His Will

If God wants our main business of life to be about his business, then we must wonder what his will, purpose, and plan is. If he is over everything, does this mean he has one overlying purpose? He controls it all, so can there really be one main plan for our lives that overshadows everything happening while we are here on this sphere of earth? The answer is *yes*.

In John 6:38-40 we see a snapshot of the complete picture of God's will when Jesus says, "For I have come down from heaven not to do my will but to do the will of him who sent me. And this is the will of him who sent me, that I shall lose none of all those he has given me, but raise them up at the last day. For my Father's will is that everyone who looks to the Son and believes in him shall have eternal life, and I will raise them up at the last day."

This verse indicates that the main goal of Jesus' life here on earth—and the paramount theme of all that happens—is that we would come to put our trust in him as Lord and Savior. That is why Jesus came to earth; why he gave himself up to be sacrificed for us; why he gave us the Scriptures; and why he performed miracles. That is why he called Saul and transformed him to the apostle Paul. And that is why we go through both the good times and experience the blessings and why we also go through the tough times and face the struggles. Everything is aimed at bringing us

18

into a relationship with him and to usher those already in a relationship with him into a *deeper* relationship.

Suffering, confusion, and unfairness can be to our advantage when they have the potential to strengthen our bond with God. The following chapters show how this is so.

Reflection Questions

1. Do you think God is really all-powerful? Why do you think he chose not to avert your tragedy?
2. Does God mean love to you? If not, what does he mean?
3. Can you say that you love God? Why or why not?
4. In what ways do you trust God, and in what ways do you lack trust?
5. What benefit is there to submitting to God's plan if it causes pain and suffering?
6. Write a prayer asking God to help you understand his love for you, and ask him to help you love him more.

Chapter 5

Misery

But he said to me, "My grace is sufficient for you, for
my power is made perfect in weakness." Therefore I
will boast all the more gladly about my weaknesses, so
that Christ's power may rest on me.
—2 Cor. 12:9

BEFORE LEAVING THE triage room, Ryanne was
hooked up to an IV that pumped fluids and drugs
designed to stop her contractions. The contractions were
coming quite frequently, about one every two minutes. This
was not a good sign. At forty weeks, contractions are great,
but one contraction every two minutes at twenty-four weeks
is something that must be stopped.

The nurses wheeled Ryanne's bed to a corner room down
the hall at the end of the labor and delivery unit. It was
furnished with her bed, two chairs, a sink, and a bathroom.
The room was tiny and dark and did not have a window. It
was cramped and confining; the thought of staying in this

room for the next ten weeks was underwhelming. But we would gladly get used to it if that meant saving our babies.

We spent the first few minutes alone, trying to comfort each other and make sense out of the dangerous situation we faced. I assured Ryanne that she did nothing wrong and didn't have anything to be sorry for. We prayed and tried to be calm for ourselves and for the babies.

Once settled in the room, we called our parents to inform them of the situation. We didn't want them worrying too much, so we tried to downplay everything as much as possible and told them that it was best to come by later. They did come by a little while later, and so did some friends. Everyone was upset, and rightfully so. Our fairytale life had just taken a horrible turn. Ryanne and I had experienced virtually no pain or difficulty in any part of our lives until this point. Sure, we had our share of family losses and problems, friend trouble, and difficulties during parts of growing up. But for the most part, things had been a cakewalk for us. Life was easy and just seemed to fall into place. We were in our mid-twenties, had successful careers, a home, paid-for cars, a great marriage, a great family, and a great life. Now, things were about to take a disagreeable turn.

The biggest obstacle we had faced thus far was getting pregnant. Ryanne had a condition that made it difficult for her to ovulate. It took us almost two years (not long by some standards, I know), thousands of prayers, and a few visits to a fertility doctor before we became pregnant. When that miracle finally occurred, *whoa*, did we feel blessed! And ... we were blessed with triplets! Now, here in this modest hospital room, our little blessings were in jeopardy of perishing. If our life had been a fairy tale, we were now facing the villain head on.

When our friends and family arrived, they witnessed Ryanne in a miserable state of existence. The contractions and the medications were already making her feel poorly, and her mental anguish was acute. It was torturous seeing my wife suffer. That Friday night was excruciating for Ryanne, but our nurse was very nice and took great care of her. It turned out I had treated the nurse's aunt in our chiropractic office. It was nice to find some common ground, and it made things more personal. I felt it might equate to more attention paid to my wife and developing children.

Ryanne was uncomfortable and had difficulty sleeping because of the IVs, three fetal monitors, and a catheter inserted in her. I helped her shift positions throughout the night in hopes of finding one that could be restful. To change positions, Ryanne held her catheter to make sure it didn't come out, while I held three fetal monitors in place on her tummy with one hand and scooped her with my other hand to flip her on her other side. Then we would go through the process of getting her pillow and bed mat in a comfortable position again. That was a restless first night, filled with struggles. Her contractions did not let up, and the pain and discomfort added to her inability to relax and sleep. How could this be healthy for our little girls if their mama was in such discomfort? I was concerned about that.

The Furthest Thing from My Mind

The next morning, Saturday, I had to leave for a while to coach my Upward basketball game. Sometime during the night I remembered I had a game, but coaching basketball was the furthest thing from my mind at the time. Ryanne's mother came up and took my place beside her bed when I left for the game. I had only slept an hour or so the night before, and it was difficult being upbeat for the kids considering all my wife and I were in the middle of. We lost the game.

On my way out of the gym I ran into one of our friends who was on staff at the church that was hosting our game. I told him the situation and asked him to please pray for Ryanne. He assured me he would. I left the gym and headed home to take a shower and change clothes. I remember that shower being the best one I had ever taken. I didn't want to get out. I just wanted to stay in there and let the water wash my troubles away while pretending the misery of my wife's situation was an illusion.

I packed a suitcase with towels, Ryanne's pillow, our toiletry items, our Bible, and some books. I made my way back to the hospital, hopeful that she had gotten some rest. But it was more of the same when I arrived at the hospital. Ryanne was still uncomfortable, terribly scared, and unrelentingly sad. She seemed glad to see me, though, and I was certainly elated to be back in her presence. The two hours I had been gone were the longest two hours of my life. I was so thankful that nothing bad had happened while I was away.

Family and friends continued to drop by, and everyone tried to keep Ryanne as comfortable as possible. Later that night after everyone left, she finally drifted off to a mediocre sleep somewhere around midnight. This left me with time to add this excerpt to my journal.

Saturday night

Yesterday and today have been the two longest and most stressful days of our lives. We may have days tougher than these in the future, but I hope not. We have been so anxious and so uncomfortable … especially my sweet wife. She really feels miserable in her inversion bed. Her gown doesn't fit, and she has to be hooked up to a catheter and an IV 24/7. She has three fetal monitors strapped to her belly with ultrasound jelly smeared all across her tummy. She is burning-up hot because of the magnesium drug pumping into her IV. They tell us that one of the side effects of this drug is that it makes your temperature skyrocket and gives you flu-like symptoms.

Ryanne can't find a comfortable position. Her back and hips hurt, she's got reflux, and she can't sleep because the meds have her so hyped-up. But we praise Jesus because our baby girls are still inside their mama's tummy. Every day counts and she's made it two days longer than she could have. God is allowing Ryanne's discomfort so the babies can remain comfortable, but it would be nicer if she was comfortable along with them. The girls don't appear to be in any distress; in fact, they seem to be thriving. Ryanne's contractions have decreased from one every two-to-four minutes to one every hour. Our main concern is that the cervix is still being dilated and the one baby's foot is still poking out.

Lord, I pray that our little baby would draw her little leg back up and turn over, and that Ryanne's cervix would close and thicken again, if it be your will. Dear Lord Jesus, I totally and completely commit the lives of my little girls and my precious wife into your mighty hands. I know and believe that you are the Master Physician, and I beg just for the touch of your cloak upon my Ryanne. Please, please, let her stay pregnant until it is safe for our girls. And please let Ryanne get comfortable and be at peace physically, mentally, and spiritually. Please let her rest. Please take away her pain, discomfort, and reflux. But if it means suffering through all that in order for all four of them to be safe and continue our girls' gestation, then please give her the strength to endure. When our little girls do come, please let them and Ryanne be completely healthy and strong.

Lord, we lay ourselves before your throne powerless and weak. We are poured out like an offering, totally empty before you. Please accept us and fill us up with your power and mercy. Be our strength and hear our prayers, O Lord, my Rock and Redeemer. In Jesus' name, Amen.

Sunday arrived. Normally we would be in church, worshipping and learning about God's goodness, mercy, and grace. This day we sat in a hospital room wondering if anything we had ever learned was actually true. Ryanne hadn't slept much the night before. Apparently, she'd had bad dreams, because when she did sleep she cried out in pain, fright, or despair. She talked in her sleep and said the craziest things. The drugs played tricks on her mind.

Changing Rooms

We changed rooms on Sunday. It was so nice going from the dungeon to a big, open room with windows. One entire wall was windows! The new room seemed triple the size of the old one, and that made a tremendous difference in the way we felt. We had better attitudes and moods with the change of scenery. It was as if we had been released from solitary confinement. If we were forced to stay in the hospital for ten more weeks, the new accommodations would make things a bit more endurable.

Things got a little scarier Sunday night:

Sunday night

Ryanne's breathing is continually getting more shallow and rapid. She still lies in the hospital bed inverted and hooked up to IVs that drip chemicals to make her uterine contractions stop. She is only 24.5 weeks pregnant with our three girls.

We repeatedly called the nurse and asked why it was getting more difficult for Ryanne to breathe, and why it hurts so badly when she tries to inhale deeply. Her first response was, "If it hurts to breathe deeply, then just don't breathe deeply." Such a response didn't sit well with either of us. Someone wasn't taking this seriously and seemed not to understand something was going wrong.

After much prodding, the nurse finally listened to Ryanne's breathing and said she would call the doctor. A few minutes later she came in and decreased the amount of medicine Ryanne was getting via her IVs.

Breathing Condition Worsens

On Monday, Ryanne's breathing difficulties continued to worsen throughout the day. The oxygen level in her blood dropped so low she had to begin wearing an oxygen cannula, the small tube worn to breathe oxygen directly into your nose. By Monday evening she was completely miserable and quite helpless. The doctor told us Ryanne had developed pulmonary edema (fluid in the lungs) from all the drugs she was taking to stop the contractions, her inverted positions, and the IV fluids. Basically, she was drowning because her lung alveoli were leaking fluid. To correct the problem she had to sit up. The medicine that stops contractions had to be discontinued because it was causing the lung problem. A new medication was given to help drain her lungs of the fluid. The doctor said this plan should work and that her lungs would be fine. Then came the kicker: He went on to say that "Up until now we have only been concerned with prolonging the pregnancy and saving the babies' lives. Now we have to turn our attention to saving Ryanne's life."

I had been concerned before, but when those words came out of his mouth my concern skyrocketed. I became much more agitated with the current situation. "Totally freaking out" is a fitting description of my state of mind after that conversation. Yes, I wanted Ryanne to stay pregnant for several more weeks for the betterment of the babies. But I didn't want what we were doing to save the babies to end up taking her life. I wanted everyone well and healthy, but that was not the way things were going.

Ryanne felt miserable; several times she said she felt like she was going to die. The doctor had just told us her life was threatened, so it was no wonder she felt that way. Each night in the hospital I encouraged her to fight the good fight. She was so uncomfortable and so sick! Can you imagine? Pregnant with triplets, lying down constantly and unable to find a comfortable position, Ryanne was hooked up to an IV, a contraction monitor, three fetal monitors, and a catheter. She couldn't get up. She couldn't even sit up. She was literally smothering.

Ryanne couldn't breathe because her lungs were filling with fluid. She was always scorching hot because the drugs to keep her contractions down gave her a raging fever. I kept rags in an ice chest for her to put on her forehead and neck to keep her cool. We had to change out those ice-cold rags every fifteen minutes because her fever was so intense.

She experienced uncontrollable tremors—shaking all over and not able to stop. Her catheter was never properly inserted, although they inserted, extracted, and re-inserted it three times. It leaked all over her and her bed. Her hair, head, neck, shoulders, and sheets were always wet because of her sweating, the catheter malfunctions, and because we used iced towels to fight her fever. The pressure from her belly was so great she could only lie in one position for thirty minutes at a time. Every half hour—around the clock—we would roll her over ... accommodating the catheter, her IV cords, her monitors, and her pillows. The most Ryanne ever slept at a time was thirty minutes, or maybe an hour at best. My poor little wife's eyes were usually open as wide as saucers. She had a dazed and panicked blank stare.

The End of the Rope

Ryanne's countenance told me that she was at the end of her rope. She was suffering through labor in an entirely different way than most women, and she didn't deserve it. She couldn't change things, and I couldn't fix them. That was a difficult realization as a man and a husband. The only thing I could do was pray for her and our little girls. *God, please.*

In the middle of those long nights Ryanne wept the most pitiful, heart-wrenching cries and say she just couldn't take it anymore. She wanted the torture to stop, but she stuck it out because she loved her girls in her womb more than she loved herself. I encouraged her to relax and try and make it just one more day … just one more day. The misery of seeing my wife in agony was too great, and it weighed on me constantly. I felt a deep and helpless pain that I realized only God could relieve. Only those who have been there can grasp the gravity of such an experience.

I kneeled beside Ryanne and held her hands and head, praying that God would give her peace in her spirit and grant rest to her body. Praise God that most of the time those prayers were answered, even if only for a moment at a time. After praying, Ryanne often closed her eyes and slept for about half an hour. Then we would start all over again with the coaching, encouraging, and praying. All of this was happening while her lungs were filling with fluid. What awful event could occur next?

Dueling Specialists

The maternal-fetal medicine specialist suggested that if Ryanne's lungs didn't clear up, and if her oxygen saturation didn't improve, he would have to take the babies via

Cesarean section in order to save Ryanne's life. He said a C-section would be necessary to prevent any damage to the girls due to Ryanne's blood oxygen content being so low. We asked how long she would be able to hold out now that she had to sit up, and since her contractions were now so frequent. He couldn't answer concretely but said that it could be minutes, hours, or even days. He stressed that every minute counted in the development of the girls. He told us we had to wait and pray that Ryanne's lungs cleared.

Next, the OB who was on call to deliver that night entered the room. He explained that delivery was inevitable soon. He tried convincing us it was in our best interest to go ahead with a C-section right now while the night was young. He reasoned that if Ryanne didn't improve, then her life would be in danger. Even if she *did* improve, it may not be a good idea to have an emergency C-section at 3:00 AM if that was when nature ran its course in the situation. He explained that it was best to have the procedure when everyone was alert and awake, and the hospital was fully staffed. Considering the advanced age of the gentleman, I couldn't help but think that he was referring to himself when he spoke about being "alert and awake."

Naturally, especially considering the fact that the OB was speaking of Ryanne's life being in danger, I really started getting nervous and tormented. So did Ryanne. Since she was feeling as if she was literally at death's door due to the pain and difficulty she experienced while breathing, the lack of sleep, the flu-like symptoms, and the constant pain in her abdomen, the OB's recommendation seemed to make sense. He and the maternal-fetal medicine doctor agreed that delivery was now imminent, but they didn't agree about the time of delivery since Ryanne's lungs were showing signs of improvement.

We were petrified to have to make the decision to deliver or not to deliver. We always thought that was God's decision. We thought that if we just prayed a little harder, God would fix Ryanne's lungs and close her cervix. After all, if our children were born tonight, they would be only twenty-four weeks and five days into gestation ... roughly fifteen weeks early. That thought alone was horrifying! The neonatologist had told Ryanne that babies born at this stage of gestation only had a twenty percent chance of survival. If they did live, they could have some kind of debilitating illness or developmental disorder. Yet, we reasoned that since God was all-powerful and since we had been living for him for so long, surely our children would be in that small percentage that made it to complete health. Because we were his children, we believed God would not allow anything to touch our children. We didn't know what to do. Finally, however, we concluded we should wait a little while and see if Ryanne's lung situation continued to improve.

Thankfully, Ryanne's sitting up and taking the diuretic medication cleared her lungs. Her oxygen saturation levels returned to near normal and her breathing stabilized. She was still in a great deal of pain, and she hurt every time she took a deep breath. Since she was sitting up, the pain in her pelvic area also returned, due to the contractions kicking back in again.

Ryanne could feel the babies pushing their way out. Her contraction monitor showed this to be the case as well, and this was exactly what we hoped would *not* happen. The maternal-fetal medicine specialist said that what happened to Ryanne's lungs was a common side effect for patients receiving the treatment she had just received. He said they had to push her as far as they could in hopes that this situation would not present. If it did, then they hoped that the diuretic and her upright position would clear her lungs.

Which it did. But now she couldn't lie down for fear that her lungs would fill up again. She couldn't take any more anti-contraction meds for the same reason. So, unless God stopped the contractions, it was only a matter of time before the babies would be born, ready or not. The maternal-fetal medicine doctor urged us to wait and not make a delivery decision ourselves.

Unfortunately for us, his recommendation and the recommendation of Ryanne's OB did not jibe. Her OB thought it was in Ryanne's best interest to deliver even though her lungs had cleared. He gave the same reasons he'd given earlier. We were in no shape to make life-altering decisions, but we felt pressured to do so by the OB. The maternal-fetal doctor encouraged us to wait, but the OB pushed us to deliver.

What Should We Do?

For an hour, Ryanne and I prayed and cried and pleaded with God to tell us what to do. Ryanne was as desperate and miserable as ever. She hurt when she breathed. Her contractions were awful. The hopelessness of the situation was weighing heavily upon her mind and heart. I was so upset I was shaking and overcome with adrenaline.

Then, a passage from a book I had read to Ryanne a few days before came to mind. It stated that God's timing isn't always our timing. Ryanne and I discussed it briefly. She said she had given all she had to give and needed this nightmare to be over. She felt she could not go on. We knew we were only buying hours and not days for our children now. According to the doctors, barring a miracle she would deliver soon, regardless of whether we scheduled the C-section or let things occur naturally. We prayed and begged God to let her and our babies make it, then we called the nurse to tell her we had decided to proceed with the delivery now.

When the nurse told the maternal-fetal medicine doctor of our decision, he came in and pleaded with us not to deliver on our own accord. He told us that since Ryanne's breathing had improved, her pain when breathing had decreased, and her oxygen saturation had increased, she needed to hold out as long as her body would let her. He stressed that he was definitely *not* in favor of doing the delivery. If Ryanne were *his* wife, he would not perform the delivery because the babies seemed fine. He said that although Ryanne felt like she was dying, she really wasn't. He assured us that she was improving and was not in harm's way any longer. He emphasized that every hour counted for babies in the womb; things could turn around. He could not tell us how long she would last before delivery, since her contractions had started back regularly, but he did assure us that he would not be placing her back in an inverted position, nor would she be getting any more magnesium sulfate, the medicine she had been taking intravenously to help stop the contractions. He admitted that she would most likely deliver much sooner than the eight more weeks that would have been ideal.

Needless to say, when the doctor left the room we were very confused. We thought God had given us an answer about going ahead with delivery, but now we weren't sure. The doctor's point about not delivering his own wife if she were in the same circumstances as Ryanne made me reevaluate our position. We talked a little more and decided to proceed as planned. The nurse had already contacted the OB, but he was at another hospital across town on a delivery call.

Meanwhile, the maternal-fetal MD brought in the neonatologist working the NICU that night. He scolded us about wanting to go ahead with the delivery. "I heard that ya'll wanted to deliver these babies tonight," the neonatologist said. "I needed to come down here and find out what was going on." He explained the severe risks for children born this early … particularly multiples. He rambled off several awful problems and disorders that develop when babies are born this early, and he told us that if our girls were born tonight, they had a very slim chance of survival.

We were confused before, but now we were utterly disoriented. We had already told our pastor and our parents that we were going to deliver tonight. They prayed over us and affirmed our decision. We were at peace. Now, our hearts and minds were suffering anguish like never before. Which way was the right way to go? All I wanted was to see my wife out of pain and my little girls born healthy. Unfortunately, these two outcomes did not seem to coincide.

We asked the maternal-fetal doctor again if he could give us a prognosis about how long Ryanne could hold out, considering that she had to sit up now. He didn't know, but he stressed that every second of gestation counts and pleaded with us to hold on and let nature take its course from here on out. He left, and we prayed through our tears of confusion and pain. We realized our decision could seal the fate or our children—not only their very existence, but also their ability to have a normal life if they survived. What a tormenting decision! Parents should not have to make these decisions. God should. Why did *we* have to decide?

A few minutes later, the OB showed up. We told him of our decision and asked his opinion. Only a few hours ago, this man had been pushing us to schedule the delivery. Now, at 11:00 PM, he suddenly changed his tune. He said that considering Ryanne's improved condition, the fact that she was apparently no longer in any danger, and the fact that the babies were not in any distress, he thought we should wait and see what happened. All three of the physicians were now in agreement with each other, and we were more confused than ever.

Wait on Him

Never have I experienced such soul-churning, agonizing personal anguish. I pray I never experience anything like it again. My mind was racing in a million directions while it played out a hundred different scenarios. For the past five days, I was mentally and physically exhausted and malnourished (I had not eaten much, and neither had Ryanne). I knew we were in no shape to make such life-altering decisions, but our hands were forced. How could our decision have been so wrong—especially since we believed it had been affirmed through our prayers?

This left us begging God to give us peace and rest and to take away Ryanne's pain. Her contractions would not stop, and her cervix would not close. We begged God to intervene in those things as well. In the back corner of my mind came an epiphany regarding the passage from the book I mentioned earlier ... the one about God's timing not being our timing. By the grace of God, that passage became clearer and clearer to me. In tears and sobs, I told my wife what the Lord just taught me.

What became clear was that the reason God's timing is often different than ours is because we never make time to *wait on him*. God makes all things happen when he desires, and not before. Since Ryanne was no longer in danger, and the babies were fine, I now knew we had no choice but to *wait on the Lord*. Ryanne was hurting badly in her chest and in her lower abdomen, and she was utterly exhausted from five days of lying flat on her back without sleep. Her sustenance consisted of Froot Loops and a few sips of soup.

It hurt me badly to ask her to wait. I could see how much misery she was experiencing. But I knew now with crystal clarity that waiting was the only way to go.

Eyes wide with pain, fear, confusion, and a million questions, Ryanne agreed to wait. She said she could tough it out for the benefit of her little girls. If anyone could do it, she was the one. She is the strongest woman I know. Ryanne is my heroine!

After we agreed to wait, we prayed again, pleading with our Lord to reverse all that had been set in motion and begging him to take care of Ryanne and our babies no matter what happened. I tried to have solid, unwavering faith, but deep down I was scared that I was walking the path of Job. I felt I could lose them all. We prayed for God's strength, presence, power, and comfort to fall upon us. We prayed for a restful night.

We called our parents back in and informed them we had changed our minds, that we were going to wait and let nature takes its course. They were totally supportive. Since it was well after midnight, we urged them and the twenty or more friends and church members who had gathered in the hallway outside our door to go home and get some rest.

Shortly after they left, Ryanne and I settled into bed and fell fast asleep. Her monitors were off her tummy. Her head was elevated. Her catheter was out. God granted us rest and gave us a peaceful sleep.

Chapter 6

Shouldn't Life Be a Bowl Full of Cherries?

BEFORE RYANNE'S PRETERM labor, the thought that God would never allow anything bad to happen to us, much less to our children, was sacred to us. We prayed the prayer of Jabez and believed it: "Jabez cried out to the God of Israel, 'Oh, that you would bless me and enlarge my territory! Let your hand be with me, and keep me from harm so that I will be free from pain.' And God granted his request" (1 Chron. 4:10). Lord, bless us indeed. Enlarge our territory.

Now our paradigm of superabundance and constant earthly divine favor had suddenly been drastically altered. We realized that we were not untouchable, and neither were our kids. That realization shook us to the core.

Our previous paradigm was flawed, and the result was incredible disappointment for us. Ryanne and I thought that we were God's chosen ones to bless and not curse. We thought God allowed everything we touched to turn to gold, and that he would never allow anything tragic like this to enter our lives. So far this had been the case, so why not now? We had lived our lives for God's kingdom and he had blessed us with great careers, families, a wonderful marriage, and financial security. Then all this happened. What had we done to deserve this turn of events?

We soon came to understand that we could never understand God. "'For my thoughts are not your thoughts, neither are your ways my ways,' declares the Lord" (Isa. 55:8). That verse of Scripture had never been more captivating, considering the situation we faced. We also started to grasp that God is not our cosmic genie, here to answer our every beck and call. We quickly found that his love is not merely manifested in earthly blessings of abundance, health, and wealth. Had we clung to only that view of God, we would have lost our faith in him as soon as our world turned upside down. Thankfully, he had shown us that he was more than that and allowed us to grasp the fact that his goodness isn't based on circumstances.

Why Does God Allow Suffering?

Nevertheless, the question remains why God allows suffering, pain, and heartache. Why does he allow these things for those who desire to follow him? This question cannot be answered fully by me or anyone because no one knows the vastness of God's mind or plan. But we are allowed some insight from his Word.

The ninth chapter of the book of Acts gives the account of Saul's conversion from an anti-Christian Pharisee to a sold-out follower of Christ. Saul was a leader among the Jews and was zealous for and very well versed in the law. He did not tolerate anyone or anything going against the Jewish law. When Jesus' followers began preaching and teaching other Jews about how Jesus was the Messiah promised in the Jewish religious writings, Saul took grave exception, so much so that he hunted down Jesus' disciples and approved of their murder. He made it his life's calling to eliminate anyone who called themselves followers of "the Way" (which is what the early Christians were called). Saul thought he was doing a great service to God, but actually he was defying everything that God wanted accomplished.

Here is the account of Saul's conversion:

Meanwhile, Saul was still breathing out murderous threats against the Lord's disciples. He went to the high priest and asked him for letters to the synagogues in Damascus, so that if he found any there who belonged to the Way, whether men or women, he might take them as prisoners to Jerusalem. As he neared Damascus on his journey, suddenly a light from heaven flashed around him. He fell to the ground and heard a voice say to him, "Saul, Saul, why do you persecute me?" "Who are you, Lord?" Saul asked. "I am Jesus, whom you are persecuting," he replied. "Now get up and go into the city, and you will be told what you must do." The men traveling with Saul stood there speechless; they heard the sound but did not see anyone. Saul got up from the ground, but when he opened his eyes he could see nothing. So they led him by the hand into Damascus. For three days he was blind, and did not eat or drink anything. In Damascus there was a disciple named Ananias. The Lord called to him in a vision, "Ananias!" "Yes, Lord," he answered. The Lord told him, "Go to the house of Judas on Straight Street and ask for a man from Tarsus named Saul, for he is praying. In a vision he has seen a man named Ananias come and place his hands on him to restore his sight." "Lord," Ananias answered, "I have heard many reports about this man and all the harm he has done to your holy people in Jerusalem. And he has come here with authority from the chief priests to arrest all who call on your name." But the Lord said to Ananias, "Go! This man is my chosen instrument to proclaim my name to the Gentiles and their kings and to the people of Israel. I will show him how much he must suffer for my name." Then Ananias went to the house and entered it. Placing his hands on Saul, he said, "Brother Saul, the Lord—Jesus, who appeared to you on the road as you were coming here—has sent me so that you may see again and be filled with the Holy Spirit." Immediately, something like scales fell from Saul's eyes, and he could see again. He got up and was baptized, and after taking some food, he regained his strength.

—Acts 9:1-19

Saul and some traveling companions were on their way to a town called Damascus to eradicate more of Jesus' disciples. On his way, a supernatural event occurred that changed Saul's life forever. He was struck blind by a great light and knocked to the ground by the majesty of the situation. The Lord then speaks to him, but Saul doesn't recognize the Lord's voice. When Saul hears, "I am Jesus, whom you are persecuting," his life is completely turned upside down. One minute he is living out what he assumes to be his calling and life, persecuting the new Christians, and the next minute he is knocked to his knees. The One he thinks he is serving has turned the tables and is sending him to Damascus to prepare for service in the new Christian church. His view of life has drastically changed in an instant. All he knows to be true about himself and his relationship with God is shaken to the core of his foundation. He is torn down, a broken man.

Not only that, but he is physically struck blind. God made Saul unable to see. He immediately became dependent on others to lead him around and to do things for him. The man who was in complete control of his own life and who held the lives of others in his hands was no longer in control.

Maybe we, unlike Saul, actually *are* living inside God's correct will. Still, that does not mean that God may not use a tragic situation to get our attention and teach us something. Maybe God sees fit to use us and our difficulties to bring glory to himself and bring others into his family.

After Saul has been blind and, no doubt, spiritually heart-wrenched for a few days, God does a beautiful thing. He reaches out to his greatest enemy and changes him into his greatest ally. God sends Ananias over to the house where Saul was staying to restore his sight and help him reconcile his relationship with the Almighty. When Saul's eyes are opened, he has a new view of the world, a new name (Jesus changed it to Paul), and a new mission. God withheld his wrath from Paul and extended mercy and grace.

Much of what we hear about God today from our pulpits is such as this story. We hear how God reaches out to us when we are totally against him, and he restores our relationship with him even when we are running in the opposite direction. The great thing about such preaching is that it is true. The apostle Paul tells us in the book of Romans that "God demonstrates his own love for us in this: While we were still sinners, Christ died for us" (Rom. 5:8). What an amazing gift! Jesus died on the cross in our place and extended mercy and grace that we don't deserve. This gift is ours for receiving Christ as our Lord and Savior.

We must be careful when we are presented with teachings that mix positive thinking with out-of-context scriptures, making it seem like if our relationship is right with the Lord then nothing bad will happen to us. Some verses do seem to make us think this should be the case, but all Scripture taken together tells another story. What about the rest of Saul's story mentioned above? What about the countless other Bible references that tell us this simply is not the case? The vast majority of God's Word details account after account of his chosen people going through seasons of pain, heartache, suffering, grief, punishment, imprisonments, and exile. The list goes on and on.

Consider Moses. He left Pharaoh's palace and fled to the desert, where he spent forty years herding sheep after he was fingered for a crime. He left the luxuries of palace life to spend lonely, dirty, and smelly years tending sheep in the desert, without a real home or family. Not only that, but after God allowed Moses to lead the Israelites out of Egypt—quite the noble task—Moses spent the next forty years walking around in circles in the desert with the nation of Israel under his leadership. He himself never made it into the Promised Land. Not quite the story of success and abundance we expect to hear much of today. But God used each phase of Moses' life as part of the divine plan.

What about Hosea, a simple farmer inspired by God to live with an unfaithful wife who repeatedly ripped his heart out? We are shown God's amazing love for his people through the example of Hosea and his wife.

How about Samson? Samson was God's powerhouse, used to defeat Philistines left and right. He disobeyed God, had his strength stripped, his eyes gouged out, and was thrown in prison and made a laughing-stock. All of this came before a terrible demise, when Samson pulled down a building killing himself and his enemies. Not quite the ending we would expect.

And suffering was not withheld from the Lord Jesus. Hebrews 12:1-3 reads, "Let us throw off everything that hinders and the sin that so easily entangles. And let us run with perseverance the race marked out for us, fixing our eyes on Jesus, the pioneer and perfecter of faith. For the joy set before him he endured the cross, scorning its shame, and sat down at the right hand of the throne of God. Consider him who endured such opposition from sinners, so that you will not grow weary and lose heart." The author of Hebrews is urging us to remember the extreme suffering Jesus endured, and to draw confidence from his example. If God Incarnate was not immune to suffering, though he was perfect, why should we expect to be?

"Not only so, but we also glory in our sufferings, because we know that suffering produces perseverance; perseverance, character; and character, hope. And hope does not put us to shame, because God's love has been poured out into our hearts through the Holy Spirit, who has been given to us" (Rom. 5:3-5). It is plain that we will suffer. Jesus says so in the gospel of John: "I have told you these things, so that in me you may have peace. In this world you will have trouble. But take heart! I have overcome the world" (John 16:33).

If God clearly teaches us through his Word that life is going to be tough, then why should we think otherwise? What a tragically devastating worldview it would be to think that the Christian life is never fraught with difficulty. Thinking that way does not prepare us for the times of trials when they do come, and these trials can instantly shipwreck one's faith. When suffering comes, many question their own salvation or the very existence of God. One could go into a state of depression, thinking that if their faith had only been strong enough they could have avoided their tragedy or—even worse—they could have turned it around.

When the Lord instructed Ananias to go to Paul and restore him, he said, "This man is my chosen instrument to proclaim my name to the Gentiles and their kings and to the people of Israel. I will show him how much he must suffer for my name" (Acts 9:15-16). Saul was God's enemy, but God loved him anyway. He loved him so much that he sent his Son to die on the cross to pay a penalty for sin that Saul could never pay. But instead of believing in Jesus and what he did, Saul continued to be an enemy of God. Yet, Jesus chose to reach out to Saul again. When Saul finally put his trust in Jesus and turned his life over to the rule of the one true God, did it mean his life would now be full of all the goodness he imagined? No! Although his new life was now life in the middle of God's will, it was going to be a life full of suffering. Where is the love in that? Where is the goodness of God?

The Love and Goodness of God is Always at the Cross

The love and the goodness of God are not only found in our worldly circumstances. The love and goodness of God are always at the cross. God knows we live in a fallen world. He gave us free will to choose not to follow his ways, and that is what we have chosen. This has caused pain, heartache, and suffering. Could he have stopped it? Of course! But he would have had to take away our free will and leave us as automatons. We would be his slaves by force, not by choice. Where is the love in that?

God knew before we were born that we would struggle with problems on this earth, problems that would rock us to the core of our being. That is why in eternity past he set in place the agony of the cross and the miracle of the resurrection so that we would have a hope and a future despite the difficulties of our past and present. No matter what misery we endure on this side of heaven, we who have made Jesus our Lord can be certain that our salvation is secure and our eternity will be forever grand because of his death on the cross to pay for our sins. Regardless of how bad life gets, nothing can change the fact that our sins are forgiven and our souls are saved. If nothing else can bring us comfort, if nothing else makes sense, and if we can't seem to understand God's reasons for allowing us to experience the pain we encounter, we can hang on to the great hope of the cross. That promise can give us the strength to persevere through trial after trial because we know that after we leave this earth we will experience complete happiness and fulfillment in God's eternal and glorious heaven.

Reflection Questions

1. Why do you think there are so many teachings about health, wealth, and abundance today that contradict the overall theme of the teachings of the Bible?
2. What are your views about God and his blessings on this earth? Have they changed due to difficulties you have faced or are currently facing?
3. Has your faith in God been shaken, diminished, or been made stronger due to your circumstances or due to other suffering you see in this world?
4. What is the greatest way God has shown his love to you?
5. Write a prayer asking God to help you reconcile how he allows tragedy and suffering while still embodying pure love. Ask God to help you trust him more, pray more, and study his Word more.

Chapter 7

The Day

And the peace of God, which transcends all
understanding, will guard your hearts
and minds in Christ Jesus.

—Phil. 4:7

WE AWOKE THE next day around 7:30 AM and immediately prayed and thanked God for allowing Ryanne
to make it through the night without delivering and for
allowing her to get some rest. She asked me to help her get
situated with a bedpan because she couldn't get up. When
she was finished, I had to pour the urine into a measuring
cup in the bathroom for the nurses to collect.

While I was in the middle of that task, Ryanne called to
me in a highly concerned tone of voice. She had her right
hand under her blanket, down by her pelvic area. Her wide,
panicked eyes told me everything before she said a word.
"Something's not right," she said. "All I did was pee. I didn't
strain or anything. I am so sorry. I am so sorry."

I instructed Ryanne to relax and told her everything would be okay. I flung the door open in a frenzied rush to find a nurse, but instead I found the admitting maternal-fetal medicine doctor who took care of Ryanne on the first day. Behind him was a lady with the portable ultrasound machine. He was making his morning rounds and was coming by to check on Ryanne. The ultrasound machine was to gauge the current positions of the babies. One glance at my wife told him everything he needed to know.

She was now experiencing a great deal of pain. Her contractions had strengthened in the past two minutes. She was holding herself and said she felt she had to hold the baby inside. The doctor put on his sterile gloves and examined her. The ultrasound nurse was instructed to get a measurement of the thickness of Ryanne's cervix and check the position of the babies as he did his exam. After his exam and the ultrasound, the doctor informed us that we would be parents very soon. He told the nurse to prepare for an emergency C-section and to call Ryanne's OB for delivery.

Picking up the Pace

The previous ultrasounds showing the baby presenting footling breech (her foot poking down with the bottom at a higher position) had now turned into a classic breech (with her bottom poking down). That was better, but still dangerous. Ryanne's cervix had definitely thinned as her body prepared for delivery. The doctors were now in a race against the clock to get the C-section performed before Ryanne went into heavy labor and started delivering the babies vaginally.

After the doctor's orders, the activity in the room escalated. Several nurses entered all at once. I had no idea why so many were in there, but they all seemed necessary because they were all doing something different. At one point, a nurse glanced down at Ryanne and asked, "Does anyone think we need to go to Trendelenburg?" I found out this meant, "Shouldn't we get her legs higher than her head again?"

The doctor inspected Ryanne and promptly gave the instructions to "pick up the pace" on the prep work. They had to get her ready for surgery quickly before she began full labor since the likelihood of Ryanne having enough strength to push for three deliveries was highly unlikely, given her exhausted condition.

What If?

A few days earlier we had a discussion with the doctor about our wishes for delivery if the current scenario presented. He asked us what we wanted to do if one of the babies decided to come vaginally and the other two didn't move into the delivery canal. Did we want to go ahead and deliver all three, or just deliver the one and leave the others inside? What an impossible decision to be faced with! Never in our wildest dreams (or nightmares) did we imagine the possibility of Ryanne delivering but still being pregnant. Of course, we never thought *any of this* would have happened. The doctors didn't give us any advice concerning which was the better path to choose. We decided to make sure that the girls stayed together and that they all be delivered at the same time.

Ryanne's bedside nurse for the day shaved her abdomen in final preparation for the C-section. A nurse brought me scrubs, a cap, a mask, and shoe coverings. She told me to put them on and have a seat in the hallway outside of the OR.

During the madness that is known as emergency C-section prep, I don't remember if I kneeled by Ryanne's bed, holding her hand, or if I was thrust into a corner of her room due to all the hustle and bustle. However, I vividly remember that we were both scared. I learned that saying you have faith in God for all things and that you have "peace … which transcends all understanding," (Phil. 4:7) and actually having them are totally different things. The truth was, I was a nervous wreck, and I didn't feel peaceful at all. I was having a hard time believing that my prayers for a good outcome were going to be answered. My wife was only twenty-four weeks and five days pregnant with our triplet girls, and that was about to end. She could not carry the babies the other fifteen weeks they needed in order to be healthy and strong. They were going to be born in mere minutes, and that scared me to death.

We Did Not Want Them Born That Day

Ryanne was much more nervous than I. It was her body and her babies. She was going under the knife. She was getting the epidural, not me. I knew that my usually calm and collected wife was really scared when she asked me to stay with her directly after surgery and not go back with the babies, as we had agreed I would do. She always said she wanted me to go with the babies to the nursery right after delivery, but things were different now.

I know that somewhere in her frantic mind she had to be thinking the same thing I was: "Where is the joy and expectancy we always assumed we would experience when our children were going to be born?" Due to their extreme prematurity, we didn't want them born that day. All the emotions one would generally have (I guess) on delivery day were 180 degrees different from ours at the present moment. We desperately wanted God to change the course of events and let our babies gestate longer.

Now, we were both thrust into the obvious reality that the pregnancy was now over. I held my wife's hand and told her how much I loved her. Our prayers turned to having the surgery to go flawlessly, for her recovery to be perfect, and for our little girls to make it. We knew God was still with us. He always is. He doesn't always give us what we want, but he does give us what we need. Why we five needed to go through this I still do not know, but I have faith that God knows.

Ryanne was wheeled to the OR. I sat in a chair just outside the doors to the OR. They would come get me as soon as she had her epidural. We had not time to call anyone. It was just us, and I was thankful for that. Although the support of our family and friends had been immeasurable and unbelievably special, it was nice to go through this as a couple alone. The entire week had been a defining point in our lives, one of those times when you look back and realize what you really have as a husband and wife. This day was a culmination of the weekend. We were in the hottest place of the refiner's fire. We needed each other—and only each other—right now. We would bask in the love and comfort of our family and friends a bit later, but now it was good to be by ourselves.

But for the moment I was alone. My wife and our babies were in an OR with people I did not know, while I sat in an empty hallway. As the hour-long minutes ticked by, I became more neurotic. I raged. *What were they doing in there and why haven't they called me in?!* My fits of uncontrollable shaking returned. I had to engage in some major praying and self-talk to regain my composure. A janitorial worker passed by and chuckled. She told me, "Calm down. Everything's gonna be all right." God's messengers of peace come in all forms. If only I could have heeded and believed her words.

Me to the Rescue

After what seemed like years, I decided to go in and find my wife. I had to rescue her! But when I stormed up to the automatic doors of the OR and they didn't open, my manly bubble burst. Apparently, the door was triggered to open from inside the OR. I dropped my head and sat down in my seat in the lonely hallway. I figured they would come get me. They couldn't forget me, right? But what if they did?

I got up, jammed my hands between the openings in the sliding doors and erupted into OR #2. No one was there. Where was Ryanne? Where was *anyone*? Was everything okay? Was I in that wrong place? Obviously, but there was no one to ask. All the nurses on the floor were with Ryanne. I looked around and saw some hustle and bustle next door in OR #3. Maybe that was Ryanne. How could I be sure? I didn't want to walk in on someone else's surgery. Everyone looked the same, green scrubs and masks and caps. If I needed something else to worry about, this was it. My wife was lost! Or was it me? Either way, it was not good.

At the climax of my paranoia, a nurse exited OR #3 and told me I could come back for the delivery. They had given Ryanne the epidural, and she was ready. The OR was unlike anything I have ever experienced. Green-clad men and women blanketed the room. Some ladies in the back wore purple. There were so many people in there, so much activity! I suppose with any surgery that is the case, and especially with an emergency C-section of triplets. Each baby needed her own set of nurses, and that added more people to the mix. A tall screen blocked my view of Ryanne's lower half. For this I was thankful. In the past I had been squeamish at the sight of blood and surgical procedures, not to mention that of my own wife and children.

Ryanne's condition was good, but she was very drugged and therefore somewhat out of it. But she was still awake. Her hands were strapped to the bed, out and away from her body, like she was on a cross. Considering the way things had gone thus far, seeing her in that position was chilling.

When I arrived at Ryanne's side and held her right hand, she noticed that her hands were strapped down. If there is one thing she cannot stand, it is to be held down. Once she realized she could not feel her legs because of the medication, and that her hands and arms were strapped down to the bed, she became agitated in short order. She asked the nurse anesthesiologist and the neonatologist, who were both standing at the head of her bed, if she could be freed. They were reluctant but agreed, with the condition that she promised to keep her hands above the screen. Little did they know that if they had not agreed, Ryanne would have superhumanly ripped the straps off of the bed. She really hates to be held down.

Sitting on a stool by Ryanne's head, I was able to lean over, hold her hand (as she squeezed mine), kiss her on the forehead and cheeks, and "coach" her through the ordeal. The entire experience was surreal. Being by her side during the delivery was much like I had imagined it. I encouraged her as she struggled through the procedure.

Although the screen blocked my view, the knowledge that my wife was being cut open was not easy to stomach. Ryanne would often wince and hold her breath because she felt such "intense pressure." The nurse anesthesiologist was professional and very nice. She kept a close eye on Ryanne and gave her more meds when the pressure became unbearable. At times Ryanne just closed her eyes. I thought she had passed out, but she was just trying to relax.

Hearing her surgeons talk about things totally not related to the procedure was odd ... and much like being in the middle of a TV show. "So, what do you think about the new policy about so and so?" "Now, your office is over there where they are doing all that construction, right?" "So, how many kids do you have?"

I couldn't help but think, "So, how about focusing on my wife and babies!"

Here Comes Number One

Then I heard, "Here comes Number One," followed by a faint cry. Our first little girl was born. Two minutes later, "Number Two!" A little cry. Two more minutes passed, and "Number 3!" No cry.

I peeked over the curtain towards the back of the room. The nurses were engaged in busyness with all three babies. No one was panicking, so I took it as a sign that #3 was fine. She was just quiet.

After the babies were born, Ryanne was crawling out of her skin and begging to know how much longer. One of the doctors informed us that it would be over in about ten minutes.

During those ten minutes, Ryanne's excruciating feeling of pressure increased dramatically. She writhed in discomfort. I heard one of the doctors say, "We better hurry this thing up because she just bent her knee." This was an indication that Ryanne's epidural was wearing off. The nurse anesthesiologist asked Ryanne if she felt any pain. "No," she answered, "but how much longer?"

Those ten minutes seemed to drag on for days. Apparently, a surgeon's ten minutes are a lot longer than other people's ten minutes. Finally, after forty-five minutes total time from start to finish, Ryanne was sewed up. The maternal-fetal medicine specialist told us congratulations on being new parents. I didn't feel like "congratulations" was the appropriate word. "Condolences," perhaps.

Chapter 8

God's Will and Our Decision

DOES GOD ESTEEM us more than himself? Our understanding of the answer to this question is pivotal in our relationship with God and our acceptance or rejection of his will. Certainly God loves us with a love deeper and more personal than we are capable of grasping. Why else would a self-sustaining God create us and allow us to live despite our rebellion? Why else would God give himself as a guilt offering on our behalf? Why else would he suffer terrible misery at the hands of the Roman soldiers? Why else would he die on a cross? The fact is that God loves us. He adores us totally and completely. But if God loves us to that extent, he certainly must love himself even more than he loves us. Does this seem right?

The Bible shares several examples where we see God protecting his glory. For instance, he gives us the command in Exodus 20:4 to not make any idols or worship anything other than himself because he is a jealous God. "You shall not make for yourself an image in the form of anything in heaven above or on the earth beneath or in the waters below. You shall not bow down to them or worship them; for I, the Lord your God, am a jealous God, punishing the children for the sin of the parents to the third and fourth generation of those who hate me, but showing love to a thousand generations of those who love me and keep my commandments." Also, Isaiah 42:8 reads, "I am the Lord; that is my name! I will not yield my glory to another or my praise to idols."

If God had our desires, wants, needs, comforts, and glory ahead of his, then he would never have made those statements. Furthermore, God may have never sent Jesus to the cross. This act of selflessness points to the greatness of God. What He did could be done by no other. Therefore, our redemption through his sacrifice ultimately glorifies God even more.

God Is Exalted Above Us

Is it a good thing that God is exalted above us? Is it good to serve a God whose primary concern is himself? The answer is *yes* to both questions.

The psalmist wrote, "For you, Lord, have delivered me from death, my eyes from tears, my feet from stumbling" (Ps. 116:8). Through Christ, God has delivered our souls from death. We will not have to live eternally separated from him if our faith is in Christ, that is, if we have confessed, repented, and given ourselves over to the lordship of Jesus. That gift of redemption in and of itself is reason enough to accept, love, adore, and submit to a God who has such a lofty view of himself. He has every right to view himself as worthy of praise, glory, and honor.

What if God allowed us ultimately to be more exalted or important than himself? How would that change the dynamic between the Creator and the creation? If we were exalted above God, the God of the universe becomes subservient to his creation. This would allow us to have some sort of control over our Creator, like a clay pot being able to tell the potter what it wants to look like, or which shelf it wants to sit upon. It is absurd to think we could have that kind of control or any kind of control over God.

If God were secondary to his creation, then his Word would not hold weight since so much of it refers to honor and glory being bestowed to him and Jesus. Jesus' place at the right hand of the Father wouldn't be meaningful or permanent. Satan's rebellion would be brushed off as a minor infraction, and all the evil that occurs in the world due to it would be discounted. In short, if God is not exalted, then our faith is futile, his Word is not true, and there would have been no necessity for Jesus to die. But thanks be to God for he is the highest of the high. Therefore, we should be happy to serve the God who has glorified himself and was willing to sacrifice his only Son in order to continue to receive such esteem, praise, honor, and recognition. God is sovereign and so is his righteous and holy will. His plans are concrete, and they will prevail. It is up to us how we will respond to them, just as it is up to us to decide how we will respond to God.

Deny or Submit

We can do one of two things in the midst of a tragedy or a life event that makes no sense. First, we can deny God and turn away from him, or second, we can submit to his will no matter how painful it may be. If we accept the premise that God is completely in control all the time, then we must realize his plans are going to be carried out whether we like them or not, or whether they are favorable to us or not. Therefore, we must decide ahead of time how we will respond to his divine will.

57

The account of Abraham and Isaac's trip to the wilderness can help us gain a sense of what it is like to choose submission to God's will. In the twenty-second chapter of Genesis, Abraham had prayed that God would give him a son by his wife, Sarah. Much later in years, she bore him Isaac, for whom Abraham had prayed.

One day, God spoke to Abraham and told him to take his son up to a mountain and sacrifice him. God had never spoken of human sacrifice before. This was new, strange, and—no doubt—disturbing. God was now commanding Abraham to kill the son he had given Abraham and Sarah in their old age. This command from God made no sense to Abraham, and it didn't fit any model he had ever heard about the characteristics of God. *Why would God give me a son and then ask me to sacrifice him?* Abraham must have thought. It didn't seem rational or logical. But our minds are not the mind of God. A situation that is perfect to him may seem like chaos to us.

We see the conundrum Abraham faced when God placed him in a situation forcing him to choose. God eventually places all of his children in situations requiring them to choose, although the events are almost never as drastic as Abraham's. We are given the option to choose to continue following God despite our lack of understanding of the situation or of his commands, or we can disobey what God says and turn our backs on him. Abraham was at such a crossroads.

The Sacrifice Was Abraham

Ryanne and I were in a similar position. No, God was not calling us to sacrifice our children. Yet, by allowing circumstances to enter our lives that did not line up with our idea of how life or God is "supposed" to be, we had the option of sacrificing our will to the pleasure of God or turning away. Abraham had the same choice. He could do as God commanded, or he could ignore the instruction.

Abraham prepared as he would for any sacrifice. He gathered his tools, wood, and provisions for the journey. Then he and his son began the hike to the mountaintop. On the way, Isaac questioned Abraham. Why were they going, and what animal would they sacrifice? Abraham continually replied, "The Lord will provide," even though he knew the Lord had already provided.

Surely, there must have been screams of protest and horror unspeakable to both father and son as Abraham bound Isaac, placed him on the altar, and raised his knife to strike his longed-for heir. Just before the life-ending blow was struck, God stopped the hand of Abraham and told him to look into the nearby bush, where a ram was caught in the thicket. God instructed Abraham to untie his son and sacrifice the ram instead. Abraham had passed the test of faithfulness, and his son was spared. God indeed provided.

Isaac was never the sacrifice in question. Neither was the ram. It was Abraham. Would Abraham allow his dream of having a rightful and full-blooded heir to be extinguished, or would he refuse to execute the command of God? Would he allow himself to be the living sacrifice spoken of years later in the twelfth chapter of the book of Romans? "Therefore, I urge you, brothers and sisters, in view of God's mercy, to offer your bodies as a living sacrifice, holy and pleasing to God—this is your true and proper worship" (Rom. 12:1). Or would Abraham turn his back on God when asked to accept the unacceptable? Thankfully, Abraham's amazing trust in God was proven true.

Abraham's response was what ours should always be. He was willing to give up his will for the sake of following God's will. Sometimes the two are intertwined, but sometimes they are not. His will is always going to prevail. Our response to his will is the only variable.

It is to our advantage that God is more concerned with his glory than with our comfort. In fact, God's love actually compels him to be more highly exalted than us, and this gives us a reason to trust in and respond positively to his will being played out in our lives, no matter what it may bring. Even if it brings bad things, the bad will end up being for our good. That is not because we deserve it, but because this brings God more honor and glory. He makes miracles out of messes. He creates blessings out of blemishes. He is always good, and he loves us so much.

Reflection Questions

1. Can you submit to God even after he has allowed or caused you great pain and suffering? Why or why not?
2. Does God really have our best interest at heart all the time? What Scripture supports your answer?
3. Are you more important to God than himself?
4. If God is more important to himself than you are, does that make it difficult for you to follow him?
5. Why is it best to have a God that thinks more of himself than his creation?
6. Why is it good to submit to God's plans even when they are difficult to follow?
7. Do you feel that God really loves you? Why or why not?
8. Write a prayer asking God to help you accept his love for you, and for you to accept his great love for himself.

Chapter 9

Our Daughters

Trust in the Lord with all your heart and lean not on
your own understanding.

—Prov. 3:5

RYANNE'S BED WAS wheeled to the recovery area. This
was a big room with several bays separated by curtains.
Apparently, this was where they took the new moms after
Caesarean surgery. Our parents and our pastor were there.
We asked the nurse when we could see the babies. The
nurse told us she could take me to see them in an hour or
so. It would take awhile to get our little girls "situated,"
whatever that meant.

Ryanne began getting the feeling back in her legs
and abdomen much sooner than expected. Two of our
friends had an unpleasant experience with their epidurals.
They both had massive headaches afterwards, requiring a
procedure called a "blood patch" to correct. Another friend's
entire body went numb for several hours after her epidural.

Considering their problems, we were happy that Ryanne recovered so quickly. We were thankful that whoever did the procedure on Ryanne had done a great job.

With her feeling coming back, Ryanne was in pain again. But all we had to do was ask the nurse for a shot to get Ryanne some relief. Those pain shots knocked her out. She was in and out of consciousness during the hour and a half of recovery.

No Visitors Allowed

The maternal-fetal doctor who had visited us the night before, hoping to convince us not to deliver that night (it worked), came in to assure us that all three babies were alive and doing as well as could be expected. He explained that their immune systems were very low, and that they needed as little stimulation as possible. He told us we were allowed to have four people besides us go in to see the babies.

We told the doctor that if their immune systems really were that compromised, we would rather not have anyone else come in and see them. He agreed that was the best idea. We knew this would be hard on our parents; they obviously wanted to see their grandchildren. But we had to look out for our babies' best interests. Besides, once the girls got well, our parents would have their entire lives to see them. The doctor said he would go out to the waiting area and give our family the update and explain the reasoning behind our "no visitor" policy.

Once Ryanne's incision stopped bleeding, and the nurse was certain there was no internal bleeding, she wheeled Ryanne back to her hospital room. The room now smelled of fresh flowers. This was a break from the normal hospital room odor. The flowers were beautiful and gave the room a nice aroma and aesthetic. Seeing the flowers made me think of the four women now in my life, all beautiful but delicate.

I don't remember how many people visited us once we were out of recovery. All I remember is the moment when the nurse told me that I could go back to see our babies. Ryanne was not yet up to wheelchair status, so after making sure she was comfortable with me leaving, I followed the nurse down the hall to the neonatal intensive care unit (NICU). Ryanne's mom stayed with her as she slept off the pain meds.

The NICU

I was still wearing the scrubs from surgery. I didn't know if I needed to wear them into the NICU, or if I could wear regular clothes. The nurse was still in her scrubs, so I figured that was the way it was supposed to be. Combine those thin scrubs with my adrenaline-crazed system, and I was shaking all over again.

Thankfully, it was a short walk from Ryanne's room to the babies. My sense of direction is not the best in the world, and that day it was worse with all the trauma and excitement. If the nurse hadn't directed me to the NICU instead of just telling me how to get there, there is a good chance I would have wandered the halls for a long time. I was a father now, and fathers don't ask for directions.

We walked up to the entry door of the NICU waiting area. Large, raised lettering hung on the wall to the right of door that read NEONATAL INTENSIVE CARE. The sign was impressive, and that in itself gave me confidence in the care of my babies. The expression "You never get a second chance to make a good first impression" never rings more true than when you are talking about the care of your children.

The nurse opened the door that led into the NICU waiting area, which was a small lobby with eight chairs, two side tables, and two counters. There was a sink on one counter with soap and paper towels. On the other counter sat two phones, one for local calls, and one for direct access into the NICU. I was to pick up the NICU phone, which rang to the reception desk inside the unit, and I was to tell the receptionist my name. They would unlock the door, and I could enter. A camera pointed directly at this phone so the receptionist could verify my identity via the monitor at her desk.

Today, however, the nurse I was with had a magnetic badge that triggered the lock of the door entering the NICU, so we skipped the protocol and walked right through. We stopped at the wash station directly inside, where there were two sinks, soap dispensers, scrub brushes, towels, disposable gowns, and surgical masks. The nurse explained that I should always stop here and wash my hands for two minutes before entering the baby area. We turned left, crossing a threshold, and I entered the NICU for my first time.

In the center of the neonatal intensive care unit, several nurses stood around workstations with computers, files, and supplies. These work docks extended all the way to the back of the nursery. Overhead skylights ran the length of the NICU and flooded the area with natural light. The walls were painted soft green and purple with sun, moon, and star borders. The floor was thick linoleum, cut with whimsical figures. Noticing the attention given to the detail of design in the nursery, I was relieved. *Surely,* I thought, *even greater attention will be given to our babies.*

I felt as if all eyes were on me. I was the proud papa of three precious baby girls—who happened to be born about fifteen weeks premature. Although I had received numerous gloom-and-doom reports from the neonatologist, I had no idea of the true severity of the situation. That is, until I finally got to see my first little angel.

"O'Sullivan #3" was tagged on her incubator. She lay face-up on what resembled a multi-functional island, the sort one would see in the middle of a kitchen. She had a ventilator tube and a stomach tube down her throat. The tape masked across her face was used to hold the tubes in place. It extended from ear to ear and from her nose to the bottom of her chin. She had two IVs and wore what looked like a Wonder-Woman wristband. She had a striped headband pulled down over her eyes. Saying she was small would be quite an understatement. She weighed only one pound, nine ounces. Her complexion was more red than yellow, but she was under bilirubin lamps to combat jaundice. She had a small T-shirt rolled up and placed under her head and neck. She also had one under her knees. She didn't really need the one under her knees; her knees were still pulled up to her chest as if she remained in utero. My guess is that she wished she were still there. I know I did.

O'Sullivan #3's head, hands, and feet seemed out of proportion to the trunk of her body. A thick plastic tent covered her bed. Two of the sides were flaps that could be raised up and down. This is where her IV lines, breathing tube, and humidifying mist tube entered her little tent. The mist tube sprayed moist, warm air into her tent to keep her skin moist. She was in her own mini steam room, but she didn't look like she was there for a resort treatment. I heard a constant vibrating noise coming from her ventilator that sounded like a train off in the distance, rolling down a track. Although she was hooked up to a lot of devices, and the majority of her face was covered by tape, this could not obscure the fact that she was incredibly beautiful. She was definitely her mother's daughter.

65

My immediate thought upon seeing my baby girl was, *I'm so sorry, baby. You are not supposed to be here yet.* The nurses in charge seemed to sense my fear. They immediately jumped in and started explaining how well she was doing, what the machines meant, so on and so on. They asked me if I had any questions. Questions? I couldn't even think of my own name.

I told our baby that her mommy and I loved her so much and that we would be back soon.

Next, we went down a few bays to see O'Sullivan Baby #2. The NICU had room for twenty-something babies, and our girls were each separated by two to three other children. Each incubator or crib was separated by curtains, which created the bays. Baby #2 looked similar to Baby #3, hooked up to the same paraphernalia—machines, lines, and wristbands. She was also gorgeous, but a little thinner. You could see her ribs too plainly. She was pulled up into a much tighter ball than Baby #3. Her nurse introduced herself and told me she would have my little girl that day. She too asked if I had any questions. Nothing yet. I was still trying to take all of this in. I hadn't had the time to make sense out of the situation, much less come up with any intelligent questions.

I told Baby #2 that I loved her so much, and that she was doing a great job, and that Mommy and I were so proud of her and her sisters.

The nurse then moved me down a few more stations to O'Sullivan Baby #1. Each incubator had a pink, thick, paper sign taped to it. The paper was folded in half. On the outside was written "O'Sullivan #1" (or their corresponding number). The inside held the place for the baby's name (we didn't have names picked out yet since they were so early), the birth date (March 1), the birth weight (#1: 1 lb, 7 oz; #2: 1 lb, 5 oz; #3: 1 lb, 9 oz.), the mother's and father's names, and their ID bracelets.

Baby #1 was being taken care of by a friend of ours. When she saw me coming over, she reached out, hugged me, and said, "You weren't supposed to come see me yet."

"I know," I replied.

She went into a little more detail with me about what was going on and what had been done for all the girls.

Upon delivery, each baby had received surfactant, a slippery substance produced naturally by the lungs to keep them open and prevent the lungs from sticking together. The quiet, train-like sound I heard was the oscillating ventilator forcing vibrating puffs of air into their lungs. This type of ventilator insured that their lungs remained open at all times, lowering the risk of the lung tissue sticking together and allowing for maximum expansion of the lungs. The headbands covering their eyes protected the eye tissue from the bilirubin lights.

The "Wonder-Woman" armband was the oximeter, which measured the heart rate and oxygen saturation of their blood. The gold-foil hearts attached to their bodies were stickers holding skin temperature monitors in place. The other two sticky squares attached to their abdomens with wires going out of them were EKG leads. The girls were getting multiple fluids and medications intravenously through two sites. All of these processes were displayed on several different monitors that would make scary alarm noises when anything was not quite right. Each monitor had a different alarm sound. Trying to figure out what was what was nerve-wracking. Some alarms meant that a medication had finished pumping. Another meant that the heart rate was compromised. Another indicated that the oxygen levels were out of balance. None were pleasant to hear because it meant something was wrong.

Our friend, the nurse with Baby #1, tried to show poise and confidence, but I could tell she was almost as shaken as I was. I imagine her trepidation was mainly because she knew Ryanne and me personally, not because our girls' situation was new to her.

After my lesson in the bells and whistles of the NICU, I told Baby #1 how much we loved her, how beautiful she was, and how proud we were of her too. She had a long way to go before she would get out there, but she could do it, I assured her. Daddy believed in her, and Daddy believed God would turn this mess into a miracle.

The nurse asked me if I wanted to stay a little while longer or go back to Ryanne's room. I told her that I would stay a few minutes more and talk to the girls. I figured that somehow I would find my way back. Actually, I didn't really do any talking to the girls, but I did a lot of staring and praying. I was in complete awe that these little girls were even alive, considering that their gestational age was only twenty-four weeks and five days. But there they were, thirty fingers and thirty toes. Amazing! I prayed and asked God to work a mighty miracle in order for these girls to make it. I pleaded for his intervention. I prayed for their strength, courage, and peace. I prayed the same prayer for my precious wife and for myself. Then I sorrowfully left the NICU and went back to see Ryanne.

By now it was 11:00 AM. Most of our family and friends were in the waiting area on the labor and delivery hall. I stopped by and told them hello and thanked them for coming. They were all very concerned, of course, and it showed on their faces. There was none of the joy or excitement one expects on delivery day. All I saw were somber gazes and tears.

The Babies Were in Trouble

Ryanne was doing well when I arrived back in her room. She was still out of it due to the pain meds, but she had full use and feeling in her abdomen and legs. That was a blessing. She and the parents in the room wanted to know how the babies were doing. "Beautiful," I replied. I hoped they could not detect how scared I really was. Seeing our little babies—who were supposed to still be in their mommy's tummy—in incubators and on life support machines was disturbing. I hoped I hid my concern well. At this point, I did not know what to tell them about the girls' condition. I could only say that they were beautiful and doing fine.

Throughout the remainder of the morning, Ryanne continued to improve. She needed less and less heavy pain medication, and that helped her get back to her normal mental state. Considering what she had been through during the past five days, I was truly amazed she was able to function and interact socially at all. She was awake, alert, and holding conversation. I think if it were me, I would have been distant and feeling sorry for myself. Ryanne was so tough, though. She did more than just "hang in there"; she was actually making it. Her daughters definitely took after their mama.

Family and friends continued to drop by all afternoon and flowers were delivered on an hourly basis. I returned to the NICU every hour to check on the girls and tell them their mommy would be up in just a little while. Ryanne got nauseous from being pushed around in the hospital bed. She was waiting until she was cleared to ride in a wheelchair before she went to the NICU.

Sometime in the late afternoon, her parents and grandparents went to eat. My parents went back to work. We had some time to ourselves again. The nurse in the NICU kept asking me what the babies' names were. I didn't know. We had not yet come up with any. We had been involved in numerous discussions about their names, but we never decided anything. We thought we had so much more time to figure them out. Now that we had some time alone, we set out to name our girls.

Since Ryanne had not seen the babies yet, she asked me what I thought they looked like. I did not have a clear answer. They certainly looked like our daughters, but to me they didn't look like a particular name. The only names we knew we wanted to use were going to be middle names— "Valerie," after Ryanne's best friend, and "Renee," after a nickname of Ryanne's from our trip to Europe during spring break of our junior year in high school. We had batted around a few ideas early in the pregnancy, but we never settled on anything definite. The same thing took place that day. We couldn't settle on any particular names.

Ryanne's parents came back from the restaurant. They brought me some take-out. I remember the food tasting really good. I was so tired of hospital food. Ryanne was cleared to ride in a wheelchair by that time, and I planned to take her to see the babies after I ate dinner. However, the time for Ryanne to see them came earlier than we expected. I was sitting at the table enjoying my take-out, when Ryanne's nurse burst through our door and frantically told us we had to get to the NICU right away. One of our babies was in trouble. She had a wheelchair, and we quickly got Ryanne out of bed and into the chair. Her dad stepped outside. As he did, two more nurses, one of them our friend who was in charge of Baby #1, shoved their way into the room and ordered us to "Get up there now!" She said we needed to move fast because the baby was very compromised.

Ryanne and I had no idea what they were referring to, but their demeanor and the frantic pace at which the nurses were getting her out of bed told us the situation was serious. We were both very scared. My stomach went into knots, and I couldn't imagine how Ryanne felt. This was the first time she'd been out of bed in five days, and it was a hurried, unpleasant, and traumatic experience. It was the first time Ryanne would see her babies and one was, perhaps, about to pass away.

I pushed the wheelchair and we followed the nurses out of the room and down the hall. Ryanne's dad, teary-eyed, gave us a look of encouragement. Ryanne gazed straight ahead, not wanting to see the tears and concern in her dad's eyes. It always makes her cry to see him show emotion. I glanced at him and bowed my head in humble appreciation for his support. He had been at the hospital almost as much as we had through this whole ordeal, sleeping in the waiting area, making food runs, doing security detail for us, and conducting business via his Blackberry. I am truly blessed to have the parents and in-laws I have.

The nurses took us the back way to the NICU, through the labor and delivery operating room where Ryanne had had her C-section just a few short hours before. We entered through two large, automatic swinging doors. We passed Baby #1 and moved towards a mass of people surrounding the station of Baby #2. It seemed as if every nurse and respiratory therapist was by her bedside. One person was manually respirating her using a hand-held air pump. Another was doing chest compressions. Baby #2 was so tiny that the nurse was using only one finger to do the chest compressions. She was pushing so hard on our girl's chest that it looked like it was going to buckle in. Another nurse listened to her chest with a tiny stethoscope, much smaller than one that might be found in a child's toy box. Others stood by and recorded vitals and notes. The doctor stood by, giving instructions on the number of breaths to give and the amount of pressure to use on the hand-held respirator. She was also giving orders for the number of chest compressions to give. Who knew you could do CPR on a baby that tiny? Who would ever want to know that you would need to?

Our first impression was that our baby was dead. We immediately started crying uncontrollably. I kneeled beside Ryanne's wheelchair, holding her, and praying silently as I watched these people try to revive my daughter only hours after her birth. I begged God to let the resuscitation work. We spoke words of encouragement to our little one through our tears, telling her that she "could do it," and that "she was so tough." Pleading with God to save my little girl, his Word and Spirit of conviction came over me like a terrible flood. All of a sudden I became intensely aware of the suffering that God himself must have felt as he willingly watched his only Son Jesus struggle for life as he was beaten to an unrecognizable form and then suffocated to death hanging on the cross. I immediately knew that if I had been God that I would have saved my son, just as I wanted him to save my daughter. Even though her death may have touched people and even brought them to salvation, as did the death of his Son, I didn't care. All I cared about was that she lived.

My heart broke as I realized I was having these thoughts about *one* of my three daughters, and that God must have had feelings a million times stronger about his one and only perfect Son, a Son he watched grow up to be a man, a Son who embodied everything the Father was and would ever be. I did not feel ashamed for praying that God would save my daughter. But I did feel unworthy to be loved by a God who sacrificed Christ purposefully for me.

As the nurses, respiratory therapists, and the doctor continued to work on Baby #2, Baby #1's alarms started beeping like crazy. A small group working on Baby #2 rushed to Baby #1. I heard someone yell, "She's dropping too!" The doctor ran over to Baby #1's bed while the remaining team continued to work on Baby #2.

In my anguish of having two daughters in cardiac arrest, I came to the end of myself. I realized that I had to give this struggle to God. I couldn't fix it, and somehow I dared to utter the most frightening words of my life: "Our Father in heaven, hallowed be your name, your kingdom come, your will be done, on earth as it is in heaven" (Matt. 6:9-10).

Never have these words carried such intense meaning as they did now. They had always just been a part of a prayer I recited every now and again in church or before a ball game. That day, the words were an act of my spiritual will, where I was giving God total control of my little girls and our lives in relation to theirs. I had prayed for them while they were in the womb, and I had prayed for them right out of the womb. But I hadn't actually committed those girls to God. I never wanted death to be his will for them, and so I never gave them to God in this manner. I wanted them to be good girls that God used for his service for years and years on this earth. I never wanted this. I never wanted to commit them to him in this way.

Repeating the same phrases again and again, "Please, God, heal my girls," and "Lord, your will be done," my sobs became greater and greater, until I was heaving. It was embarrassing when I think back, to be so broken and weak before my wife (for whom I was supposed to be so strong) and in front of all of these strangers. But I couldn't help it. My will was broken and was now in complete submission to God. It was both a horrible and yet a wonderful place to be. It was horrible because it was possible that God's will was to take them away. It was wonderful because being in the center of God's will is always a perfect place to be, and what if God's will was to heal them?

Another doctor came and stood beside us, since the other doctor was now at Baby #1's bedside tending to her. This doctor, the same one who was in Ryanne's delivery, became the overseer of the procedures being done on Baby #2. All of a sudden, a few of the nurses stopped working on her and walked away. The doctor said, "Well."

"Well, what?" I asked. "Is she gone?"

"She's okay. She made it," he replied.

Hallelujah!

The nurses cleared out and went back to check on their other babies. About that time, two of our pastors rushed through the doors coming from the OR. Their faces flushed and their breathing quickened, it was obvious that they had received a phone call and rushed to our side. They looked as concerned as we felt. I told them through my tears that we almost lost two of the girls, that their heart rates suddenly dropped, and they had to perform CPR on both to revive them. My sweet wife just sat in her chair staring straight ahead. She was still a bit dazed and confused from the medication and from the events of the past several days. I looked at her. Her face was as white as snow. She was feeling faint and asked for a cold cloth for her forehead. No wonder. This was the first time she had seen the babies.

Naming the Girls

One of the doctors came over and explained that with infants born so premature sometimes the scenario that had just played out happens unexpectedly. Their heart rates will suddenly drop for no reason and with no warning. Usually it takes only mild stimulation to the bottom of the foot or to the spine to bring the heart rates back up, but occasionally they have to do chest compressions and manual ventilation. She also said that sometimes it is necessary to give epinephrine shots into the heart, which is what they did to Baby #2. The epinephrine is a shot of adrenaline administered directly into the heart muscle through the chest wall to stimulate the heart to beat faster.

The doctor explained that as they were working on Baby #2, Baby #1's heart rate started doing the exact same thing. She did not need a shot of epinephrine, though. It was difficult to witness what we witnessed, and knowing that my little girl had to get a shot right in the chest made it all the more difficult to bear. Our little baby had been through so many traumas already, and she was only a few hours old.

Ryanne and I knew those two girls were very close in the womb. Naturally, they were all close, but Baby #1 and Baby #2 were the closest. Ryanne's ultrasound pictures revealed that these girls were almost touching heads. They were so close that at first it looked like they were going to be Siamese twins. On most of the ultrasounds, it looked like the crowns of their heads were combined. Ryanne and I intuitively felt that the response of #1 was due to the fact that she sensed that her sister was in trouble. In utero, Baby #3 was off by herself compared to the close proximity of Baby #1 and Baby #2. Maybe that is why she didn't have an episode at the same time that day. Anyway, that was our reasoning.

Ryanne and I remained in the NICU after our ministers left. She had a difficult time seeing the baby from her wheelchair since the incubator unit was so tall. With all the strength she could muster, Ryanne stood up in order to get a good look at her child. Ryanne told our baby girl how much she loved her, how amazingly beautiful she was, and how proud she was of her for putting up such a hard fight. I wouldn't wish this situation on anyone, but seeing the mother of my children and my beloved wife gather herself after watching her child almost die and then speak such powerful, encouraging words was probably the most inspiring scene I have ever witnessed. Forget *Braveheart*. Forget *Legends of the Fall*. Forget *Hoosiers*. Forget *Rocky*. This was as real and amazing as it gets. As the big, strong father, all I felt like doing was lying on the floor and crying. But I took the cue from my fragile but resilient wife and stood up to be the rock our little girls needed.

Ryanne could only stand up for a short time. She was still weak, queasy, and wobbly. I wheeled her over to see Baby #1. We sat by her bedside as Ryanne tried to comprehend the magnitude and gravity of the situation. It seemed that by her silence, she was absorbing the reality that our three daughters were actually here and were definitely way too early, a reality I was still trying to grasp myself.

After a few minutes of sitting by Baby #1, Ryanne stood up to get a better look. Ryanne whispered and told her how proud of her she was and what a sweet, pretty, and strong little girl she was. We told the baby that she was going to be just fine. She only needed to hang in there and allow God to heal her.

After spending some time with Baby #1, I wheeled Ryanne down the corridor of the baby beds to the far end of the nursery. Here in a quiet corner lay Baby #3. She was the first one I saw on my first trip into the NICU, and now she was the last one Ryanne saw. Ryanne immediately stood up from her wheelchair to catch a glance of our third child. She was the biggest of the three at one pound, nine ounces. Considering what had happened with the other two, Baby #3 became the "big sister" even though she was actually the youngest. Ryanne and I gave her the same encouragement and love that we had given the other two girls. We exhorted her to continue being a strong girl and to be there for her sisters. We told her that we loved her and then we left the

NICU so that Ryanne could get some rest. She was very tired and nauseated after such a scare.

On the way back to the room, we took the route that led us through the lobby waiting area. Several of our family and friends were there. We assured them the girls were fine, although two of them had given us a fit for a few moments. We tried to keep the mood light and said that we knew we were in for several more years of them "acting up." We told everyone we wanted to be alone for a little while, and we went back to Ryanne's room.

The nurse helped me get Ryanne back into bed. I pulled a chair up beside the bed and suggested that we now name our girls.

Psalm 139:13-16 says:

> For you created my inmost being; you knit me together in my mother's womb. I praise you because I am fearfully and wonderfully made; your works are wonderful, I know that full well. My frame was not hidden from you when I was made in the secret place. When I was woven together in the depths of the earth, your eyes saw my unformed body; all the days ordained for me were written in your book before one of them came to be.

This Scripture proved to me that God had our girls' names picked out way before we did. We just had to seek him to find out what the names were supposed to be. There was a song on the radio during this time by a band named Selah, which contained the lyric, "You knew my name before there was time. Oh, this was just part of your glorious design." How true. The names God gave the girls and the names we figured out were as follows:

Baby #1 is Reece Valerie. Ryanne loved the name Reece, and Valerie is the name of Ryanne's longtime best friend. We named Baby #2 Vivian Grace. Vivian because we thought it was a really pretty name for a pretty little girl, and Grace because we recognized that it was only due to the grace of God that she was still with us after the episode only moments ago. Baby #3 is Sophia Renee. We named her Sophia because it is such a precious name, and Renee after a nickname given to Ryanne by friends while we were on a trip to Europe in high school. Our friends in Europe told us that Renee was the European equivalent to Ryanne. Probably not true, but fun. As I called out these suggested names to Ryanne, our eyes welled up with tears, which gave way to all-out crying when we realized we were making one of the most important decisions that parents could make in the naming of children.

Throughout that first evening, our parents came by at different times. We took these opportunities to tell them the names of our little babies. Ryanne and I cried each time we told someone their names. I never thought that in our culture naming a child was that big of a deal—until it was up to us to name our babies. The pride we felt once we had cemented our children's names was immense. The thought that those combinations of letters would help define our little girls on this earth was amazing. You know someone when you recognize their face, but you really know someone when you recall their name. Proverbs 22:1 says, "A good name is more desirable than great riches; to be esteemed is better than silver or gold." Now, they had names that would allow them to leave their indelible mark on this world.

Later in the evening, I went back to the NICU to visit the girls and to tell them their names. The nurses came to say hello and check on me when I arrived. Each one asked if we had come up with names, and I could finally tell them we had. I told Sophia her name first. She seemed to like it, elegant as she was. Then, I moved down to Vivian's bed, her graceful, royal highness. I finished up with Reece, who was already too cool for Spartanburg and probably destined for NYC. I tried to be the big, strong Daddy, but I got choked up while talking to each of the girls. It was a big deal for me to speak their names to them. I told the girls that Mommy was getting better, that we loved them, and that they were all so strong and were doing such a great job. I told them we were so proud of them and that we would be back soon. It was difficult leaving them in there alone. If only we could have had them in the room with us! But this was the way it was supposed to be.

Ryanne and I went to see the girls a couple of times during the night. The NICU was like Vegas … always light, always open. In between visiting the girls, we slept some. Ryanne wasn't very comfortable from her surgery, and our minds were racing. This was not how we thought things were going to turn out. Our babies should still have been in the womb, not in mist tents under bilirubin lights in the NICU. When our minds were quiet we prayed for Reece Valerie, Vivian Grace, and Sophia Renee—and we did not forget to pray for ourselves.

Chapter 10

Our Greatest
Example

WHERE DOES ONE turn for inspiration, guidance, strength, and peace when the world is falling in, and when things are not going as planned? The church answers "Jesus." Jesus is God, and God is omniscient and omnipotent, all-knowing and all-powerful. "In the beginning God created the heavens and the earth" (Gen. 1:1). He made it all. He knows it all. He knew our girls would be born too early. He knew that Reece and Vivian would have those scares that first day, and he knew what we would name them.

God also knew what we would wear today. He knows what burdens we carry due to scars from childhood or from a bad adult relationship. He oversees all of it—the good and the bad. He sets all things in motion, and everything that is has its fullness in him. As Hebrews 2:10 puts it, "In bringing many sons and daughters to glory, it was fitting that God, for whom and through whom everything exists, should make the pioneer of their salvation perfect through what he suffered." Ephesians 1:22-23 testifies to this as well: "And God placed all things under his [Jesus'] feet and appointed him to be head over everything for the church, which is his body, the fullness of him who fills everything in every way." Jesus is King of everything, and all things are completed in him. All things are made whole in him because he "fills everything in every way."

This idea of wholeness, fullness, or completeness is a grand concept to grasp because it reminds us that without Christ, life and its experiences are not complete. It reminds us that there is a total picture we may not yet be seeing, but one day we will see it in its fullness. When Jesus was in the tomb, the disciples did not see the big picture. They were in the middle of the story, though they thought they were at the end. But God gave them the full photo on the third day and for the forty days thereafter when Jesus rose and continued to minister before his ultimate ascension into heaven before their very eyes. It is important to remember that we are not yet seeing a completed portrait as we journey through the ups and downs of life. We may not see the fullness of a situation, but we can rest assured that God is in control over all.

God's Plans Are Not Always Pleasant

Since God's will is unchangeable, his plans never waver and will always prevail. Sometimes these plans are not pleasant for us to endure, but for those who love God, they are always for our ultimate good. His plans are always carried out to bring him glory and to increase his fame, as well as for the eternal benefit of his beloved children. We must believe both of those truths because we will face challenges in life that seem to defy both realities. How could suffering make God more popular and how does suffering benefit anyone?

Think about Jesus. He is God. He has always been and will always be. "The Son is the radiance of God's glory and the exact representation of his being, sustaining all things by his powerful word. After he had provided purification for sins, he sat down at the right hand of the Majesty in heaven" (Heb. 1:3). "In the beginning was the Word, and the Word was with God, and the Word was God. He was with God in the beginning" (John 1:1-2). He knew from eternity past he would have to leave heaven and come to earth in bodily form, be born in a manger, and live a less-than-glamorous life. He would have no place to lay his head, and he would be rejected by his family and scorned by his religious leaders. His life would be a life of intense public service and scrutiny, and he would be falsely accused *by his own people* after living a perfect life. After being accused, he was beaten beyond recognition and finally brutally killed by being hung on a cross. Jesus knew all of this, yet he was willing to be born into the human condition and follow his Father's will. He realized that abiding by God's will would bring him earthly persecution, which would only last for a little while but would end in his eternal glorification.

The verification of this is found in Philippians 2:6-11:

> Who, being in very nature God, did not consider equality with God something to be used to his own advantage; rather, he made himself nothing by taking the very nature of a servant, being made in human likeness. And being found in appearance as a man, he humbled himself by becoming obedient to death—even death on a cross! Therefore God exalted him to the highest place and gave him the name that is above every name, that at the name of Jesus every knee should bow, in heaven and on earth and under the earth, and every tongue acknowledge that Jesus Christ is Lord, to the glory of God the Father.

What an amazing example Jesus is to us to submit to God's plans willingly. So much so that in the verse just before this passage, Paul exhorts believers with these words: "In your relationships with one another, have the same mindset as Christ Jesus" (Phil. 2:5). Through the inspired hand of God, the apostle Paul realized that Christians would need some help understanding our roles in the drama of life. He wanted us to experience life with a sense of humbleness and perseverance, not entitlement. He wanted us to know that though we will experience hardship, our reward will one day be eternal life and all the benefits of heaven.

Accepting God's Plan Willingly

We tend to avoid impending pain and suffering as often as we can, but Jesus knew the torture he was to endure and he accepted it as part of God's general salvation plan. In the Garden of Gethsemane, on the eve of Jesus' crucifixion, Jesus said, "Father, if you are willing, take this cup from me; yet not my will, but yours be done" (Luke 22:42). Jesus in his humanity did not want to go through what his divinity knew he was about to suffer. Yet, he submitted. Not that we should rush into tragedy or look for ways to be persecuted. That would be foolish. But when heartache, tragedy, persecution, and calamity do make their way into our lives, we need not be surprised or offended. If God himself did not avoid it while here on earth, why should we expect to? We must be prepared to face our difficulties and meet them head-on with the full confidence in Christ.

While the nurses worked feverishly on Reece and Vivian, I prayed for God's will to be done. And I honestly meant it. Deep down, though, I think the main reason I could pray for God's will was because I believed God would do just what he did—save them. They didn't die. His will was for them to live, but what if it hadn't been? What if I knew that his will had been for them to die that day? Would I have boldly prayed "Your will be done"? Was my acceptance of God's will based solely on my belief that his will was only for their earthly healing, that his will was what my will was?

How about you? Are you accepting the cards you have been dealt and relying on God's provision, peace, strength, and power to get you through? Or are you fighting him every step of the way, angry that life has been unfair, unkind, and cruel? Do you accept God's plan willingly as long as it is pleasing to you, or do you trust in his will no matter the earthly outcome? Do you blame God, or are you content living according to his will right now? Jesus was our greatest example of how to submit to God even when it is not easy or pleasant.

Hebrews 12:1-2 gives us perfect insight into this: "Therefore, since we are surrounded by such a great cloud of witnesses, let us throw off everything that hinders and the sin that so easily entangles. And let us run with perseverance the race marked out for us, fixing our eyes on Jesus, the pioneer and perfecter of faith. For the joy set before him he endured the cross, scorning its shame, and sat down at the right hand of the throne of God." The writer of Hebrews tells us plainly that Jesus knew the outcome of his life would be the cross, scorn, and shame. Beyond this he also knew he would be glorified *after* the scorn and shame. He knew his heavenly Father was faithful and would see him through the tragedy to the triumph.

You may say, "But he was Jesus. I'm not him. I'm not as strong. I'm not omniscient." That is true, but you do have a bit of omniscience because you have the authority of Scriptures, which tell us, "We know that in all things God works for the good of those who love him, who have been called according to his purpose" (Rom. 8:28). If this verse is true—and it is—then we can have the same attitude of Christ; we can persevere through God's sometimes difficult will. We can be encouraged by the truth of Hebrews 10:23 that God is constant: "Let us hold unswervingly to the hope we profess, for he who promised is faithful."

We can hold to that hope and have the attitude of Christ because we are assured of future joy, just as Jesus was. The Lord obtained a resurrected body and eternity in heaven; our future is the same. We will live past death and spend eternity in heaven if Jesus is our personal Lord and Savior. It is imperative that we, just as Jesus, keep joy in the forefront of our minds and hearts at all times. God's promise of joy and hope are like the carrot held out before the donkey, spurring him on. Sometimes the cart we pull gets mighty heavy, and the roads of life can be bumpy and long, but with the joy set before us we can endure.

Reflection Questions

1. Why do you think Jesus asked for the cup of suffering to pass from him?
2. How does it make you feel that the Lord Jesus went through the torture of the cross when he didn't have to?
3. Do you think it was necessary for Jesus to suffer as he did? Why or why not?
4. What benefits have come from Jesus willingly going through with sacrificing himself on the cross?
5. How has this chapter made you see life's struggles (or your own situation) differently?
6. Where will you find strength to endure your challenges?
7. Write a prayer of thanks to Jesus for willingly suffering through the agony of the cross on your behalf.

Chapter 11

Sacrifice

The earth is the Lord's, and everything in it, the world, and all who live in it.

—Ps. 24:1

THE NEXT MORNING we awoke and immediately went to see our girls. They were all pretty, tiny, and cute, and doing as well as could be expected. Ryanne was feeling a little better and that was good. She had been through so much the past few days. I was amazed how well she was recovering physically and emotionally.

Our parents called to check on us, but we kept to ourselves for most of the morning, alternating between going to see the girls and hanging out in our new room. They had moved us to a recovery room on the fifth floor, three floors up from the NICU. We weren't happy about having to move because we were farther from the girls, but we couldn't stay in the labor and delivery area anymore. Both of these activities were over.

Changing rooms was not a lot of fun. We had so much stuff to move. I had brought a lot of our personal items from home because I thought Ryanne was going to be in the hospital for a few months. We had food, snacks, books, games, an air purifier, and a humidifier. There were clothes and towels and toiletries. Our new room wasn't as large as the old one, but it was still much better than the abyss of our first room. At least the new room had a window.

In the early afternoon, Mom and Dad offered to take me home to get us some clothes. I asked Mom to stay with Ryanne, and asked Dad to drive me home.

It was difficult leaving my four ladies. Our home was fifteen to twenty minutes away, and I knew I would be gone for at least an hour. But we all decided it would be good for me to clean up. Ryanne was all for it. I think it was her way of taking care of me. Besides, deep down, we all felt we were shining in the light of God's favor. We knew in the depths of our hearts that yesterday's scares were merely that ... yesterday's scares. We had no doubt that from now on our little ones would be great. So I went home.

Dad and I stopped by Burger King on the way. I remember my Whopper being really, really good that day. I ate and talked on the phone as Dad drove. I had several voice mails to answer from other family members and friends. It was weird telling people I was now a father, because at this point it was not a very joyous announcement. I was sad that Ryanne wasn't pregnant any longer. It meant a long, tough road ahead for our little girls. I hated feeling sad about being a parent. It was so wrong, but I couldn't overcome it.

We arrived home, and I headed up to take a shower. Dad asked if he could change the sheets on our bed, or fold some laundry, or do something. He wanted to help. "Anything would be nice," I replied. I had Dad hold my cell phone while I was in the shower just in case we got a call from the hospital.

Cleaned up in new clothes, with more in my overnight bag, we headed back to the hospital. We were about eight minutes down the road when my phone rang. It was a number I didn't recognize—a number that would soon be burned forever in my mind. Ryanne's mother was calling from a hospital line. She told me we needed to hurry because Reece was "having a hard time again." She sounded pretty cool about it, but I made sure that Dad double-timed it back.

As Dad sped through town, a flood of emotions hit me. I was so scared for my little girl, and I was upset that I was on the road and not at the hospital with my wife. It hurt me that I had been selfish and left Ryanne alone. Why did I leave when she couldn't? Why did I go anywhere when my girls were so critical? How could I leave them? How was Ryanne holding up? Was she with our Reece? Was this like yesterday? Would this happen each day? That doctor wasn't kidding when he said we would be in for a roller-coaster ride. Those thoughts and many others bombarded my brain as we returned to the hospital.

Traffic intensified as we neared the hospital. Roadwork blocked some lanes, so Dad took the back roads to bypass the snarled mess of cars and cones. I'm not sure we arrived any faster, but we had to try. Dad pulled up to the front entrance of the hospital and let me out. I jumped from the Suburban and ran to the stairs. Luckily, the NICU was just one floor higher. Skipping several steps in an all-out sprint, I reached the second floor and the NICU. They buzzed me in, and I ran to see my baby and my wife.

Déjà Vu

Entering the NICU, I looked back to the far bay where Reece was located. Ryanne was sitting in front of Reece's bed, holding a tissue and crying. Several nurses, a respiratory therapist, and a doctor were working on our firstborn baby girl. It was a replay of the scene from the day before. I kneeled beside Ryanne and told her how sorry I was for leaving her. She said she'd only been there for a few minutes due to having a moronically slow orderly in charge of wheeling her down to the NICU.

The scene unfolded just like the day before. After watching them do chest compressions and manual respiration on our baby for about two minutes, the doctor kneeled down beside Ryanne and me. Her disposition was not comforting. They had been trying to revive Reece for nearly twenty minutes. The baby's potassium levels had suddenly skyrocketed, and this caused her heart rate to decrease significantly enough for them to have to do the resuscitation. Next, the doctor said the worst phrases my ears had ever heard: "Everything we are doing ... it's not working. She is not responding." This mortifying statement was followed by the saddest question I've ever been posed: "Do you want us to continue?"

Tears rolled down our faces. Ryanne and I looked at each other in shock, disbelief, and fear. We couldn't believe this was happening to our baby. We had a problem comprehending a question of such magnitude. We didn't respond for a moment, thinking, *Could this be it for Reece? Is God allowing our baby to die? The doctor must be wrong.*

Finally, I answered, "Yes. Please continue for a few more minutes." We thought that maybe, just maybe, a few more chest compressions would work. Maybe one more shot of adrenaline and a couple more fervent, soul-wrenching prayers would make a difference.

They didn't.

After a couple more minutes, the doctor leaned down and told us that their efforts were futile. Reece's heart monitor showed a heartbeat only when they performed chest compressions. When they stopped the chest compressions, a flat line showed. She was gone.

Terrible Despair

Unspeakable grief immediately filled our hearts. The doctor said she was sorry, but sometimes these things happened to premature infants. She continued explaining. We began sobbing.

I was still kneeling beside Ryanne. We held each other as I buried my face in her arms and wept uncontrollably. I couldn't understand what had just happened. The first baby God blessed us with had been suddenly taken away. Reece was gone, and the pain of losing her was unbearable. No warning. No time to prepare. In the span of a few minutes, our baby was gone. How could this be?

Through her sobs, Ryanne kept repeating the phrases, "This is terrible. This is so terrible." Indeed it was. Even in the depths of my own pain, I could not pretend to grasp the pain a mother must feel at the loss of her baby. Who could? I will never know the despair she felt, and I am not sure that I could handle it if I did.

The nurses and the doctor cleared out and pulled the curtain around us to give us time alone. Ryanne and I clutched each other and gazed on our sweet baby girl's body. We knew it was now vacant and void of her tough, little spirit. In my dismay, I uttered the simplest of prayers in hopes of bringing us peace, no matter how small. "Our

Father in heaven, hallowed be your name, your kingdom come, your will be done, on earth as it is in heaven. Please, God, take care of our little baby Reece. We love you. Amen."

I hate to admit this, but it was so hard to say the words "I love you" to the person who had just taken my precious baby from me. Although I may have been mad and confused and upset, I still loved God because he first loved me. My faith in his substitutionary death and resurrection allowed us to be with Reece again one day. This brought me hope, and I loved God for that hope. I quickly came to the realization that although in this life we will have trouble, heartache, and suffering, the love of Christ trumps them all.

The nurses came back in the bay after a few minutes of allowing us to be alone. They asked us if we wanted to hold Reece. Unfortunately, we had never been given this option while she was alive. We were told that preemie babies didn't respond well to touch. How awful that it wasn't until our little Reece had passed away that they asked us if we wanted to hold her. It is a very hard thing to say, but I was completely mortified at the thought of holding her. I deeply regret that I did not take the opportunity to hold her. I missed that chance, and I will never have it again on this side of heaven. At the time, though, I was so shaken up that the thought of holding my deceased baby horrified me. All I could think about was how angry I was that Alice Cooper made a song entitled "Dead Babies," and that I had ever heard it and seen the video of him performing it. It was a strange thing to think at a time like that, but that is what went through my mind, nonetheless. Thankfully, Ryanne did want to hold Reece. What a blessing to have such a loving and courageous wife.

The nurses took as many cords and wires out of Reece as possible, swaddled her in a blanket, and handed her to Ryanne. My cries quickly turned to sobs again. They became heavier and heavier as I watched Ryanne hold our sweet, precious daughter. Truly, I have never felt such sorrow and never known such pain. The image of my wife's heartbroken face as she gazed upon the tiny face of beautiful Reece, first born and first to pass away, will be burned on my heart for the remainder of my life. It was a portrait of tragedy.

This was not the way we had envisioned things happening. Wasn't the first time a mother holds her baby supposed to be joyous? How completely backwards. Ryanne's firstborn was deceased the first time she held her. As a husband and father, I felt guilty for ever getting her pregnant because she had to suffer through this misery.

Ryanne and I cried and cried, rocking our baby for several minutes. We alternated talking to Reece and talking to God. "We love you so much, sweet, pretty Reece." "God, we love you, but why?" "Reece, we love you." "God, thank you for making sure our little Reece will never suffer again." Such a jumbled web of thoughts and emotions flowed through us. The suddenness of it all was overwhelming. Ryanne asked if I wanted to hold her, but I just couldn't. How horrible of me. How terrible I feel now! But I couldn't bring myself to do it, not even after seeing Ryanne hold her. I don't know what my problem was.

Ryanne didn't want to give Reece back to the nurses; neither did I. We both knew that once we did, that was it. We would never hold her or see her again. We already missed her so badly, and she had only been gone for moments. We no longer had three daughters.

After several minutes, we realized we couldn't hold our precious Reece forever. We had to lay her to rest. As the nurse entered our bay, I leaned over and laid my hand on little Reece's body, kissed her forehead, and told her that I loved her so much. Ryanne squeezed her tight for the final time, and we let the nurse take our baby daughter.

What complete anguish I felt and saw on the face of my wife as she handed our baby to the nurse. She asked if we wanted to see Reece again after they cleaned her up and got her into a dress. We couldn't handle the thought of having to say goodbye again, so we thanked the nurse and told her no. She also asked if we wanted the staff to take pictures of Reece. We declined. We felt it would be terrible having pictures of the baby when she was not alive when they were taken. Thankfully, the nurse didn't listen to us. She took pictures, anyway. We were not thinking clearly at the time, and we wouldn't give anything for our picture of Reece today.

Ryanne and I were taken to the transition room, a room where families stay when they are preparing to take their baby home. It's like a hotel room, but it is in the NICU. The parents stay overnight and take care of their baby while under the supervision of the NICU staff. For us, that room was only a place to cry, hold each other in private, and attempt to gather ourselves emotionally before telling our parents and friends the bad news.

We stayed in the room for about twenty minutes. Then we decided it was time to tell everyone. On our way out, we stopped by Sophia's and Vivian's beds and told them how much we loved them and that their little sister was in a better place and was watching over them. We told them we would be back soon, and we made our way out of the NICU.

As we exited the NICU into its adjoining waiting room, we saw that a large group of our family and friends had gathered and were quietly talking among themselves. It's possible they could tell by our tear-streaked faces and sad eyes what had happened. I am sure our demeanor was somewhat similar to the day before, when we'd almost lost Vivian. Today was much different.

I had explained to Ryanne that I would do all the talking so that she wouldn't have to. I addressed the crowd as strongly as I could.

"Reece just passed away." Everyone's heart dropped, eyes widened and teared up. They seemed to be in as much shock as we were. Things kept going from bad to worse, and they were transitioning quickly. We had no time to prepare for the storm that came our way. Life was grand, and then five days later Ryanne was no longer pregnant and one of our children was gone.

Chapter 12

Perseverance
through Suffering

I N ROMANS 5:3, the apostle Paul states, "Not only so, but we also glory in our sufferings, because we know that suffering produces perseverance." Paul was explaining to the Christians in Rome how they have hope in the glory of God because of the grace he has extended them. He then explains how they must also rejoice in their sufferings. Christians in Rome were under a tremendous amount of persecution, including beatings, torture, being boiled to death, being crucified, and so on. Paul was letting them know that it was to their benefit to rejoice in these trials because they would produce perseverance, the ability to continue on towards a goal despite hardship.

This is a tough lesson to learn or even comprehend. If a friend has been thrown into an arena to fight a lion because he was a Christian, then I think it may be difficult to rejoice in that situation just for the sake of learning to persevere. But this is essentially what God was saying through Paul. We can be certain that if God thought it important enough to include in Scripture, then it must be an important lesson to learn. Considering this, let us dig into *perseverance* a little deeper.

First of all, we must remember that the suffering Paul is referring to is not self-inflicted. The Christians to whom Paul was writing were not suffering due to some sin they were involved in, but rather they were suffering because they were following God's will. They were living the life God wanted them to live, and that is why they were being burned at the stake. With that in mind, we must come to the realization that living according to God's plans does not always mean our lives will be free from care. It could mean—as it meant for many lives in the first century—that we lose our life. This is an important point we cannot forget as we continue in our Christian walk.

Health and Wealth?

There is so much "health and wealth gospel" preached today that is not accurate according to the Bible. Sure, God wants us to be happy, but there is no guarantee that just because we live according to his principles, or just because we give our lives to his lordship, that we will get everything we wish for and that we are immune from misfortune and harm. If we search Scripture, we learn that the opposite is usually true.

Guarantees of health and wealth were never given to Jesus. He never owned a home. He had no place to lay his head. His friends abandoned him. He was arrested unjustly, tortured, and killed. This was not a model of a pleasant life to be following God's will so closely. However, Jesus persevered to the end and now sits at the right hand of the throne of grace as our King and Lord forever.

And what about the author of the Romans passage we are referring to in this chapter? Paul lived all-out for God, fully in the divine will, and yet the apostle was beaten several times, shipwrecked, tortured, and imprisoned until he died. He submitted to God's plans and look where it got him ... nowhere, as far as earthly success is concerned. There was no health and wealth gospel for Paul. Still, as a Christian, he realized this earth was not where he held his citizenship. His citizenship was in heaven, and he lived every day as such. He said, "That is why we labor and strive, because we have put our hope in the living God, who is the Savior of all people, and especially of those who believe." (1 Tim. 4:10). This is the hope that motivated him to persevere during the most trying of times.

The author of Hebrews writes:

> Therefore, since we are surrounded by such a great cloud of witnesses, let us throw off everything that hinders and the sin that so easily entangles. And let us run with perseverance the race marked out for us, fixing our eyes on Jesus, the pioneer and perfecter of faith. For the joy set before him he endured the cross, scorning its shame, and sat down at the right hand of the throne of God.
>
> —Heb. 12:1-2

These verses encourage us to keep going despite the doubt, fear, persecution, loss, disease, sin, and other obstacles we will face in our lives. The New Testament writer assures us that we will encounter things we must "throw off" in order to continue running the race and living out the Christian life. The author offers Christ as the ultimate example of one who endures pain and punishment because he was aware of the coming glory. Like him, we are assured of heaven in our future so we can have the strength and fortitude to suffer through whatever we are called to suffer through. Whether it is the loss of a child, health issues, family heartache, or whatever, we know our end is only a beginning.

James 1:2-4 echoes this sentiment by teaching us to "Consider it pure joy, my brothers and sisters, whenever you face trials of many kinds, because you know that the testing of your faith produces perseverance. Let perseverance finish its work so that you may be mature and complete, not lacking anything." Several crucial points are revealed in these verses.

The first one is that we will face trying times. My wife and I faced the situation involving a premature delivery of our girls and losing Reece. That was quite the challenge, but this was not the only challenge we would ever be called to face in our lives.

The second crucial point is that while we will face trying times, we should be joyful about them. Wow! How hard is that? I get mad when the water isn't immediately hot in the shower. How much more difficult will it be to be joyful in the midst of true hardships—like loved ones getting sick and dying, financial troubles, homelessness, starvation, and persecution?

The third one is that we go through trials so our faith will be tested in order to develop perseverance. Think of Job, from the Old Testament story mentioned earlier. If it wasn't for the refiner's fire, gold would never be purified. You have to bust open the rock to find the diamond inside. What does Paul say in 1 Corinthians 9:25? "Everyone who competes in the games goes into strict training. They do it to get a crown that will not last, but we do it to get a crown that will last forever." He uses the example of athletics to make a point about spiritual matters: athletes don't get into shape by happenstance. They go through tough workouts. Shouldn't we expect to go through trials in order to get in shape spiritually and be made into the image God desires?

The fourth point is that perseverance through trials completes and matures Christians. Suffering has a purpose, and God uses it for our benefit in the end. According to 2 Peter 1:6, perseverance leads to godliness: "... and to knowledge, self-control; and to self-control, perseverance; and to perseverance, godliness." According to Romans 5:3-5, perseverance leads to the development of character: "Not only so, but we also glory in our sufferings, because we know that suffering produces perseverance; perseverance, character; and character, hope. And hope does not put us to shame, because God's love has been poured out into our hearts through the Holy Spirit, who has been given to us."

If we grasp these concepts, then we are able to persevere and God is ultimately glorified. If we do not grasp such truths, then our faith collapses when tragedy arises and all hope is lost. Therefore, persevere. Don't give up. Press on ... and on ... and on.

Reflection Questions

1. Why is it difficult to praise God and be joyful during challenging times?
2. How are we supposed to have peace when our world turns upside down?
3. Who is our ultimate example for perseverance?
4. What lessons about perseverance are you learning in your life now or from difficult times?
5. How do you see yourself using these lessons to help others?
6. Is it easy or difficult to persevere through God's plans for your life? How so?
7. If all of God's plans were easy to follow, would we need perseverance?

Chapter 13

A Shot to the Heart

A time to weep …

—Eccles. 3:4a

BACK IN THE room, I helped Ryanne into bed from her wheelchair and crawled in with her. I held her, and we cried until every single tear ran out. We were so incredibly sad that little Reece had passed. We were in such disarray and shock. We couldn't make heads or tails of the situation. The only thing that kept us sane was our knowledge that our little girl was in heaven, and that because of our personal relationship with Jesus, we would eventually be with her for eternity. Our hope in eternity helped us so much. We were thankful we still had each other, Sophia, and Vivian. But that didn't erase the pain we felt by missing Reece so desperately.

Our pastor, DJ, knocked on the door after an hour of letting us be alone. He came to ask if we felt like having our parents come in now. We were ready. When they came in, they tried to comfort us. We tried to be strong, and we tried to be a comfort to them. We were not successful. Flowers began arriving, expressing sympathy for our loss. Our room held flowers of congratulations and flowers of sorrow—for the same twenty-four hours!

The remainder of that evening is a blur. I don't remember much of anything except the hours I lay in bed holding Ryanne as we cried together, prayed together, and read the Bible. I am sure we went down to see Vivian and Sophie, but as for details or specific conversations, I have no recollection. All I remember is emptiness and pain.

We tried to sleep that night, but it didn't go so well. Thankfully, Ryanne's nurse that night was a longtime patient at my office. She was sympathetic and took great care of Ryanne while respecting our need to be alone. When we awakened during the middle of the night, we took the opportunity to visit our little angels in the NICU. It was nice going down in the middle of the night. The nursery was calm and quiet. The staff always explained how the little girls were doing. They would go over numbers and medications with us. We were still the new parents on the block, so most of their stats meant nothing to us as of yet. I don't recall many condolences from the hospital staff regarding our baby's passing. Of course, it was 4:00 AM, and my mind wasn't exactly all together. Someone could have baked us a chicken and I probably wouldn't have remembered.

In any event, we spent some time with Vivian and Sophie in the quiet of the early morning hours. It was difficult seeing Reece's bay empty. An absolutely awful thought entered my mind the first time I glanced down there: "One down, two to go."

Satan is known as the Prince of Darkness. During this dark time in my life that coincided with the deep darkness of the night, he shot an arrow of discouragement straight to my heart and mind. That thought really shook me up. Was that to be our fate, to leave the hospital with no children? It just couldn't be, I reasoned. God wouldn't allow that to happen. At the same time, I was concerned because I now realized I knew nothing about the future plans of God. I thought Ryanne would carry our babies to near term and they would live long, happy, and fulfilling lives. That was not the way things had turned out.

After spending time with our little ladies, Ryanne and I went back to her room and slept in each other's arms for a few more hours. Sleep was good. It took us out of the nightmare of our reality.

Chapter 14

Character

I CONSIDER MYSELF blessed to be the product of a broken home. My parents divorced when I was very young, one or two years old. They also remarried while I was still a toddler, so the "broken home" was healed, and I had the good fortune to grow up experiencing the love of two different families. The opportunity to balance the time and love of two sets of parents, grandparents, siblings, and others has no doubt helped shaped my personal character. Character, the soul-substance of what we are made of, is formed through our life experiences. Ryanne and I were in the middle of some more "character-building" circumstances.

One of my dads, Gary O'Sullivan, has worked for most of his life on the sales side of the cemetery industry. For years he worked at a cemetery-funeral home business in my home town. After Reece died, he took me back to his old place of employment and walked me through one of the most difficult decision-making times of my life. I signed my name on a contract I never imagined I would ever have to sign. It was for the burial of my child. When the pregnancy test comes back positive and you realize you are going to be a father, your mind never conceives that you will have to bury that child. But I was now making those preparations.

Dad knew all the right people to make the experience as quick and easy as possible ... as if *anything* about this experience could be considered quick and easy. Looking at burial plots and a tiny white casket for your baby has to be the definition of difficult. I count it a blessing that Dad knew how to navigate that process. At the funeral home, the conversation centered on the date, time, and proceedings of the burial service. I was asked if I thought we should have the funeral so soon (two days later) because of the bleak status of Vivian. She was not doing well. The funeral director was insinuating that maybe we should push the service back a few days in case she also passed. The thought of us waiting for another of my children to die was disturbing. I said that we would schedule the service as we had planned. If we had to change it, then we would cross that bridge when we came to it. I certainly was not trying to entertain the thought of losing another one of my daughters.

Dad made the process go smoothly. While away from the hospital, I received no urgent phone calls like the day before, and I made it through the saddest business transaction of my life.

Ryanne was anxiously awaiting my return. She was ready to comfort me because she knew I had just done such a difficult thing. She was upset that I had to do the entire funeral planning without her, but I was glad she couldn't go. A mother should never have to see her baby's casket, much less while she still has two babies in the NICU.

As soon as I returned, we went directly to the NICU to see our baby girls. We would have liked to sit in Ryanne's room for the remainder of the day feeling sorry for ourselves, but we had to persevere for the sake of Vivian Grace and Sophia Renee. Only by the grace of God were we able to do so. He was building character in us as he saw fit, and it was the most difficult thing we had gone through. We know it was only through our faith in God's goodness that we were able to make the treacherous journey with him instead of abandoning our faith to follow our own path. We could have abandoned the Lord, but he would not forsake us. He never leaves us or changes. We are the ones who do the running.

Grade IV Bleeding

When we arrived at the NICU, the doctor on duty wanted to talk to us, and his countenance suggested he didn't have good news. He informed us that premature infants have chest X-rays daily to check for lung expansion, proper alignment of the IVs and tubes, and to make sure the child has not developed pneumonia. They also have weekly head ultrasounds to view the brain. Preemies are at a high risk to develop bleeding disorders of the brain, particularly in the lateral ventricles where the cerebrospinal fluid develops.

Today's ultrasound showed that Vivian had a Grade IV bleed, the worst she could have. They didn't know when or why it happened; they never know. The doctor told us what a Grade IV bleed meant for Vivian's health outlook; the prognosis was not good. This was especially difficult to accept after just making Reece's funeral arrangements.

A Grade IV bleed meant that Vivian had a severe stroke in her lateral ventricles—so severe that the blood actually leaked out into her surrounding brain matter. If she survived (not something you want to hear about your two-day-old baby daughter), she would more than likely be severely mentally and physically handicapped. Her condition could be so extreme that she would never be able to breathe without a ventilator, and she would never be able to eat except through a feeding tube. Vivian's heart and lungs could grow strong, but it was unlikely her brain condition would ever improve. Permanent brain damage had been done and that Vivian would always be in a "vegetable" state, constantly hooked up to life support.

The doctor suggested it was all right if we wanted to turn off her life support, to assure she would never have the life he had just described. He assured us that whatever decision we made would be the right one.

Before leaving, he told us Sophie had a small Grade I bleed, but it should self-correct with no complications or further damage. Was that good news or just not-so-bad news? Everything was so confusing. As he left us to our thoughts, the doctor closed the curtain around the three of us in order to give us some time alone with Vivian and some time to think. Ryanne and I held each other, and we wept again. We assured our sweet little Vivian that she was going to be fine. This was just another chance for God to use her as a platform to perform a miracle. We truly believed that because we knew the medical team had no hope. Vivian had to have a miracle, and we felt confident God would provide one in his time. At the same time, however, we were scared that if she did miraculously live, how bad would she have it?

Would God choose to let Vivian live with feeding and breathing tubes always attached, and no ability to communicate or move on her own? Would she live only to spend her life in a coma? It was possible, and that possibility was not easy to cope with. We prayed this would not be her lot, and we asked God to completely heal her.

What is Faith?

We were thinking positive thoughts, but in the back of our minds we were both scared that Vivian might not get through this challenge. We weren't sure if we had faith or if we were trying to work up a confident outlook on life. Where does one end and the other begin? Where do the two meet? Why did we have to continue this exercise in building character? Hadn't we been through enough? Hadn't we shown ourselves true?

The dictionary defines *faith* as "a belief in the value, truth, or trustworthiness of someone or something." It says that being positive is being "very confident, absolutely certain; not negative." The Bible says that "faith is confidence in what we hope for and assurance about what we do not see" (Heb. 11:1). To me that sounded just like having a positive mental attitude; therefore, faith and positive thinking seemed to coincide—until now. They began to differ for me when I realized that faith is where we place our trust in the trustworthiness of God for him to bring about whatever it is we are hoping for.

Being positive about a situation only necessitates that our minds and personal abilities factor into the equation. Being positive does not depend on God. Ideally, Ryanne and I would have had complete faith and positive attitudes, but considering all that had happened in the past few days, our faith *and* our positive thinking had been shaken. We were beginning to think that God might allow something else bad to happen to our babies and us, so we had a difficult time believing that Vivian would be healed.

Our positive outlook was really just positive talk. We had no ability to change the situation ourselves. Only God could heal her. Love, attention, and encouragement could not. Two cornerstones of our lives were rocked—faith that

God would answer our prayers as we wanted (the majority of pop-culture faith boils down to this), and our ability to positively bring about desired results.

Hebrews 11:1 is not referring to unseen material or earthly blessings. When the writer of Hebrews says that "faith is confidence in what we hope for and assurance about what we do not see," he is referring to the hope of Israel—the Messiah. The Messiah is what the New Testament refers to when considering the hope we have as Christians. Jesus was the Christ, the heir of David, and the fulfillment of the Old Testament prophecies. He was the summation of the Law and the Prophets. Therefore, when the writer of Hebrews mentions that "faith is confidence in what we hope for and assurance about what we do not see," it is possible he is implying that faith is when we are certain that God is who he says he is, that Jesus is the Messiah, that his Word is completely true, that one day what we do not now see will be made certain, and that we will see the fulfillment of God's kingdom.

Realizing that truth has made all the difference in the world to Ryanne and me. It takes God's promises from focusing on the temporal to the eternal. Even though one of our daughters had passed, and the other two had bleeding disorders of the brain, the faith we had in the completeness of Jesus' work on earth to save our souls made our lives bearable. If our faith in earthly circumstances had failed, at least our faith in our heavenly destiny had not.

God's Word Is True

What is the best way to make it through life when circumstances do not seem fair? Have faith in and be positive about the truth of the gospel. In the New International Version (NIV) of the Bible, Jesus is recorded as referencing *truth* 107 times. John 8:31-32 reads, "To the Jews who had believed him, Jesus said, 'If you hold to my teaching, you are really my disciples. Then you will know the truth, and the truth will set you free.'"

Although we were horribly scared and confused, Ryanne and I were still free ... free from the doubt that God was anything but who he says he is, free from being worried about the assurance of our salvation, free from the thought that we would never see our little Reece again. We were free in the truth of the gospel. We realized that the Father loves us, and that he sent Jesus the Son to die in our place so that we could have a relationship with him, the one, holy, true God. Our strength of character was not based on earthly circumstances but on our firm belief that God's revealed Word is true.

On the topic of character, the book of Acts records that "the Berean Jews were of more noble character than those in Thessalonica, for they received the message with great eagerness and examined the Scriptures every day to see if what Paul said was true. As a result, many of them believed, as did also a number of prominent Greek women and many Greek men" (Acts 17:11-12). We see from this portion of Acts that character can be directly related to seeking and having faith in truth. If affliction produces perseverance, and perseverance produces proven character, then part of our perseverance must involve sticking to our faith in truth. All our lives we say we believe in the supremacy and goodness of God, and we will forever be his followers, and that nothing can snatch us from his hand. Why, then, when the going gets tough, when life seems to make no sense, and when God seems unfair and unkind, don't we stay true to him? Isn't that when our character is proven the most? In those times, we see where we stand in our relationship with God. We will find out if we really have faith in him and the real promises of his Word, or if we have only been true to *our* interpretation of God. We find out who we are, and those around us find out who we are, as well. Our witness for Christ is solidified or it crumbles.

The key to proving our character during such disheartening and perplexing times is by being like the Bereans long before we reach the hardships of life. The verse from Acts says that this group "examined the Scriptures every day." This was the reason given for them having "more noble character." In the midst of a crisis, it is too late to test what we believe and see if it is true, much like it is too late for a basketball player to practice his free throws in the midst of an end-of-game foul shot situation. The relationship we have with our heavenly Father leading up to the crisis is what will get us through.

When I was a little boy, my dad (this time I am referencing David Ivey) tried to get me to go on a roller coaster. I was afraid to try. He said, "Have I ever made you do anything that would hurt you?" The answer was always no. I knew from our past experiences that he would not put me in a situation that would hurt me, so I knew I could trust that fact enough to go on Space Mountain. It's the same way with us and God. If there has never been a relationship due to our lack of trying, or if we have never taken the time to invest in discovering what the Scriptures teach about God and about our lives as they relate to him, then when we *must* know, we really do *not* know. What we thought to be true may not be the real truth. This has the potential to destroy our faith if it has never been strong. If our faith has been weak or one-dimensional leading up to a trial, then there is the potential that it will be destroyed because of the trial. Our character will definitely be proven during trying times.

Therefore everyone who hears these words of mine and puts them into practice is like a wise man who built his house on the rock. The rain came down, the streams rose, and the winds blew and beat against that house; yet it did not fall, because it had its foundation on the rock. But everyone who hears these words of mine and does not put them into practice is like a foolish man who built his house on sand. The rain came down, the streams rose, and the winds blew and beat against that house, and it fell with a great crash.

—Matt. 7:24-27

If the foundation of who we are is solid and built on the Rock of Ages, then we will be able to stand strong through the torrents of life.

Reflection Questions

1. On what is your strength of character based?
2. Do you think there is any other way to develop character and faith other than "trial by fire?" If so, what are some other ways?
3. During difficult times now or in the future, do you imagine your character will be proven strong or lacking? What makes you think so?
4. How have the challenges of your life helped shape the person you are today?
5. What are some aspects of your character you are glad you have, due to making it through rough challenges?
6. Can you see yourself being able to help others during their trying times because of what you have learned in your life experiences?
7. Do you think it is worth submitting to God's will when it is contrary to your will, in order for your character to be developed more fully?

Chapter 15

She Lies by a Beautiful Tree

I will go to him, but he will not return to me.
—2 Sam. 12:23

WE WERE TOLD to inform the doctors and nurses if we made any decision regarding Vivian's life support. They would continue with her regular treatments as if everything was normal—until we gave them further notice. Ryanne and I didn't even have to discuss her life support. If we would not consider cutting off life support on sweet Sophie, who couldn't live without it, then we surely wouldn't terminate life support on her sister. Yes, Vivian's circumstances were drastically different, given the trauma to her body during the resuscitation the prior day and the brain hemorrhage, but who were we to give the order to turn off her breath? Our thoughts were that if God wanted her gone, then he would take her. Until that time, we had to give her a fighting chance and an opportunity for divine healing.

We wouldn't judge others who may choose another way to look at things. Personally, we could not bear the thought of willfully giving up our child or giving up on her. We told Vivian to continue being the tough, strong, little girl she was and that God would heal her. We had hope, and we would project only that assurance to our little Vivian.

The doctors told us that Vivian was scheduled to have ultrasounds every three to four days to monitor her brain bleeds. We couldn't wait until the next ultrasound because we wanted to see how much better she was and how our prayers had been answered.

Still upset, we made our way down the room to spend time with Sophia. She looked so big and strong compared to Vivian. We could not help but tell her to "take care of your little sister." Vivian seemed much more frail than Sophia.

We went to the waiting area to share the latest edition of sad news with everyone. We knew we looked upset because everyone had a change of countenance as soon as they saw us. I broke the news about the girls' conditions, recounting what the doctor had told us regarding Vivian's long-term outlook. Needless to say, everyone was heartbroken.

Our pastor asked if he could talk to me for a minute in private after he had walked us back to our room. I took Ryanne inside the room, and stepped back out into the hallway with DJ.

"Has the doctor spoken with you and Ryanne about the possibility of taking Vivian off life support or giving a 'Do Not Resuscitate' order?" DJ asked.

"Yes," I answered both questions.

DJ assured me that whatever decision we made would be the right one. "Nowhere in the Bible does God give us any indication about what to do in a situation concerning life support machines. The girls probably wouldn't be here today had they been born twenty-five years ago. The technology to keep them alive wasn't available then. I want you and Ryanne to know that you have my full support, whichever route you choose."

"DJ," I said, "We intend to give Vivian the same fighting chance we're giving Sophia. We intend to keep her hooked up to everything."

A Man in Love with God

I stepped back into our room to find Ryanne kneeling by the bed. She was crying and pleading with God to heal our little Vivian. After getting down beside her and holding her as she prayed, I helped her up and into the bed, where we continued our tearful petitions to God. We cried and prayed until both tears and prayers seemed to run out. Who knew we could create so many tears?

Our parents showed up at our room one hour later on the dot. They made attempts to cheer us up and encourage us. "God has healed others just like this," they said. "What can we do for you?"

Our only response was "Pray." Our girls desperately needed prayer, and so did we. We were so weak physically, mentally, and spiritually. We could tell that our parents wanted to take our pain onto themselves. They would have fixed everything for us if they could have. We felt the same way about our little girls.

Later in the evening, two of our pastors and their wives stopped by the room. They had been to a banquet for local church leadership at a nearby church. They spent over an hour with us that night. They told stories about the banquet that made us laugh, a seemingly impossible feat at the time. Their visit helped us escape from the reality or our grim situation. The Bible tells us that we are to encourage and refresh one another. Our friends did that for us.

Before leaving that evening, Pastor DJ asked if we had anything we wanted said, read, or sang in Reece's service on Saturday. I asked DJ to relay a story from 2 Samuel 12, on the loss of King David's son:

David pleaded with God for the child. He fasted and spent the nights lying in sackcloth on the ground. The elders of his household stood beside him to get him up from the ground, but he refused, and he would not eat any food with them. On the seventh day the child died. David's attendants were afraid to tell him that the child was dead, for they thought, "While the child was still living, he wouldn't listen to us when we spoke to him. How can we now tell him the child is dead? He may do something desperate." David noticed that his attendants were whispering among themselves, and he realized the child was dead. "Is the child dead?" he asked. "Yes," they replied, "he is dead." Then David got up from the ground. After he had washed, put on lotions and changed his clothes, he went into the house of the Lord and worshiped. Then he went to his own house, and at his request they served him food, and he ate. His attendants asked him, "Why are you acting this way? While the child was alive, you fasted and wept, but now that the child is dead, you get up and eat!" He answered, "While the child was still alive, I fasted and wept. I thought, 'Who knows? The Lord may be gracious to me and let the child live.' But now that he is dead, why should I go on fasting? Can I bring him back again? I will go to him, but he will not return to me."

For much of my life this passage has been dear to my heart. Here is a portrait of a man in love with his son. But more than that, David was a man in love with God. King David prays, fasts, and weeps before his Almighty God for the healing of his sick son, but an earthly healing never comes. The king's son dies. Then, instead of going insane or turning his back on God for not granting his request, David stops grieving, gets cleaned up, eats, and worships God. He doesn't question the Almighty. He doesn't get angry at God. He worships.

We can see David's complete faith that God and his plans are sovereign and good, although his plans did not allow for David's son to live. King David also had complete faith that one day he would see his son again in heaven. We see his confidence in that knowledge when he says, "I will go to him, but he will not return to me."

Ryanne and I were only able to cope with this tragedy because of our faith. We had not really lost Reece; we were merely separated from her for a period of time. She would not return to us, but we would go to her. The beautiful thing is that the next time we see her, time itself will no longer exist. We will be with her for eternity. We can't wait for that!

Leaving the Hospital

Our friends left, and our parents came back in. They offered to do anything to make our lives more pleasant. We assured them we were fine but just really tired. We were also sad beyond measure and scared beyond belief. However, we tried not to show those emotions because we didn't want our parents worrying more than they already had.

When our parents left for the evening, Ryanne and I went down to see the girls. They were so sweet and fighting so hard. I became a stronger person witnessing their and their mom's toughness. I knew I would never give up on anything again and that I would always give every endeavor my all—just like my daughters and my wife. What an inspiration they were—and still are—to me!

The girls were so pretty and so tiny in their little beds. My hand went all the way from their bottoms to the tip-top of their heads. When they were fully stretched out, they came only half way up my forearm. Ryanne and I prayed over both of them, begging God to heal their brains and bodies. We tried hard to believe he would.

The next day, Ryanne was discharged from the hospital. It was difficult leaving. We would both be gone and away from the babies. Before, if I was gone, Ryanne was still nearby. Now, they would be there alone, without either of us. Even if we were only gone a few hours at a time, we were going to miss them so much.

It was also difficult to leave the hospital because we were returning to an empty home, with an unfinished nursery that held only two cribs instead of three. My parents had taken all of Reece's things back. We were going home from the hospital with no babies. Our house would be too quiet and too lonely. The most difficult reason for leaving was that it meant that we had to attend the funeral of our baby Reece.

The ride home was sad, slow, and deliberate. We didn't talk much. We didn't know what to say. Ryanne was feeling better, but she was not ready for any Andretti-like driving tactics by yours truly. I took it slow and easy, and she was happy about that.

Pulling into our neighborhood, we noticed three pink balloons on our mailbox. We thought it was a nice gesture. It reminded us that even though we were in the midst of a tragedy, our girls were born to us. We were parents, and that was a good thing. Some people never have an opportunity to say that, but we did. Since Ryanne had a condition that made it difficult for her to ovulate, we weren't sure if we would ever have that opportunity. We had tried to get pregnant for a year and a half before finally seeking the help of a reproductive endocrinologist. Two months of tests, hours of prayer, and two low doses of fertility medication later, and Ryanne was pregnant with our girls. The doctor told us the medication had less than a one percent chance of contributing to multiple births. We considered it a miracle and a blessing that Ryanne got pregnant with three babies. We were thankful to be parents, even though it had not been the great experience we had expected.

Back at Home

Our parents had dropped off our belongings from the hospital the night before. This included lots of plants, flowers, and balloons. The house was filled with pretty plants and the sweet smell of fresh flowers.

Ascending the stairs to our bedroom was a monumental task for Ryanne. The most number of stairs she had walked since surgery were three. Sixteen was more difficult and more time-consuming, but she mastered them. Emotionally, we dreaded going up the stairs. The nursery was up there, just to the right. Thankfully, seeing the nursery was not as sad as we expected it to be. When we saw it, we realized how thankful we were that at least we had two cribs. Vivian and Sophia were still with us. We were filled with hope that they would be coming home soon. For Reece, we had the blessed assurance that she was in the arms of Jesus. Those thoughts gave us the strength to continue on.

Getting cleaned up and ready for the funeral service was a somber experience. We had been to funerals before and had to pick out clothes to wear. But deciding what to wear to the funeral of your newborn daughter was a task beyond burdensome. I think it was so tough because, as Ryanne pointed out, when we wore those outfits in the future, we would think back to this sad, sad day.

Next, we had the arduous task of going into the nursery closet and picking out a toy to lay with Reece's casket. It was painful entering their empty room and choosing a stuffed animal—not for Reece to play with but to be buried with. It was one of the most disturbing things I've ever done. Reece would never play with that stuffed animal. She would never come home to this house, which we'd bought with her in mind. Ryanne and I had moved into our new, larger home just two months prior to all of this happening because we needed more room with three girls on the way. Difficult as it was, I picked up her stuffed Disney Mickey Mouse and brought it with us.

Our friend and one of the pastors at our church, Kevin Harrison, picked us up in Ryanne's grandfather's Cadillac and drove us to the cemetery. We had the funeral service set up so that everyone would be seated and ready for the service to begin when we arrived. We just wanted to arrive, sit down, hear the service, and get back to the hospital as quickly as possible. In retrospect, it would have been better to grieve together with our family and friends and to focus a bit more on Reece's service. But our sorrow was so great that day we didn't want to talk with anyone before or after the service. We wanted to be alone and with our other two girls.

We knew the only comfort we would experience that day was back at the hospital with Sophia and Vivian. *At least we have them*, we kept thinking. Most parents who lose a newborn don't have two other newborns. They lose the one and that's it, no more kids. We considered ourselves blessed to have Sophie and Vivian. That blessing did not numb the pain of Reece's passing, but our two other daughters, precarious as their health was, provided a bright ray of light on that dark day.

The Day of the Funeral

It was a short drive to the cemetery, about ten minutes from our home. Ryanne and I embraced one another in the back seat of the car. We cried. Kevin drove. No one talked. The day of the funeral was a beautiful, sunny day. The previous day it had rained buckets. But on this day God allowed the clouds to break and reveal gorgeous blue skies, temperatures in the 60s, and a gentle (and sometimes ferocious) breeze. As we turned into the cemetery, we were astonished by the number of people we saw. We thought most people would consider the event a family-only graveside service. It was humbling to see all the support, and we felt honored that our little daughter's life touched so many people in just one day.

Kevin pulled the car to a stop near the service tent. Reece's grave is near my grandfather's. They are beside one of only three trees in the entire cemetery. The graveyard itself is set back from the main road. It is a beautiful and quiet piece of property.

Our parents and siblings stood near our parking space ready to greet us. They were not seated as we expected. Most were crying. We tried to be strong, but surely they saw through our façade. The family followed us to the seats under the tent. We held our heads low, not wanting to make eye contact with anyone. We knew all eyes were focused on us. It was only a short way, but it seemed like such a long walk through the crowd, past our baby's white casket, to our seats on the front row. Although this day was supposed to be completely about Reece, Ryanne and I hated feeling that we were on exhibition.

Reece's casket was very small. It had pretty, pink baby roses laid on top, and it sat on a small table that was covered with white linen.

I don't remember much about the service—only a few details. It was horrifyingly dreamlike. I remember holding my wife's hand as we both wept, trying to hold back complete sobs. I remember Pastor DJ reading and explaining the Bible passage about King David and the loss of his son. I remember almost breaking down as DJ read, "Can I bring him back again? I will go to him, but he will not return to me" (2 Sam. 12:23).

Although Ryanne and I longed for an extended life with Vivian and Sophia, we now also longed for death so we could be with Reece again. I remember the breeze picking up so greatly at times that I feared the tent would blow over on us. I remember praying hard for Vivian's and Sophia's healing. I remember the strength of my wife. I remember loving her so much more than I had ever loved her. I remember her loving me so much more than she had ever loved me. I remember DJ reading the poem he wrote in honor and memory of Reece.

"Tuesday's Child"
Tuesday's child was full of Grace,
Then Wednesday came and took her from this place.
Our heads held low and our hearts held broken,
We hold each other with trembling hands
and soft words spoken.
Where now shall we find comfort when only
silence follows our "whys?"
To whom can we go when strength
fades in our goodbyes?
My answer slowly comes in the deepest
moments of despair,
The Spirit, He gently speaks to me in a heart
language of care.
Oh, now I am reminded that hope from
suffering is never torn,

Because of another child who rose on a blessed
Sunday Morn.
On a cross He took death's sting and felt
her greatest pain,
That we might have peace with death
knowing her only as our gain.
This child we mourn today will surely be seen again,
By those who know the One who took away
death's bitter end.
Hope lies with our Savior, so tomorrow we can face,
Because we know this Tuesday's child now lives
forever in the fullness of
His Grace.

I remember being sick with grief about my little Reece being in that casket. I remember thinking that parents shouldn't have to bury their kids. I prayed that the non-Christians in the audience would not think that God is not good or that he doesn't love us or our kids. I remember praying for people's relationships with God to be reconciled or to materialize for the first time. I remember missing my little Reece so badly and hurting more than I ever thought possible.

DJ closed the service by praying. He stepped over and hugged the family and expressed how he hoped he had done an adequate job. He did much more than that.

Ryanne and I stood up. We walked to the table and placed Reece's Mickey Mouse on the table next to the casket. Then we left the service. We left our family and friends. We left our firstborn baby in the middle of a field only five days after her birth.

Kevin drove us home. He asked if there was anything he could do for us. We declined. We wanted to get changed and get back to the hospital as soon as possible. We were afraid to be away from Vivian and Sophia.

We wanted to change our clothes and set out for the hospital before people came by the house. No such luck. We didn't even make it up the stairs before a car pulled into our driveway. We weren't too happy about that since we told our pastors and our family to keep everyone away. Luckily, it was Ryanne's sister. She brought Ryanne's nephew, Seth, because he had drawn us a picture he wanted to give us. Seth was seven years old. He was all dressed up like a little man, with a tie and everything. He was visibly upset. Seth was a big kid with a very tender heart. Ryanne, misty-eyed, thanked him for the picture. Seth gave Ryanne a hug and then he left with his mother.

We changed, made a sandwich for the road, and took off to see our other two babies. We both felt that the girls must be as upset as we were. Of course, they may have been happy for Reece, because they knew she was now with Jesus forever and she would never suffer again. There is no reason little babies can't have knowledge like that. That knowledge gave us all hope.

Hope

THE EARLY CHRISTIAN church, much like the church today in certain parts of the world, experienced persecution like none we have ever seen in the U.S. Believers were routinely put out on the streets, thrown in jail, tortured, and put to death. Despite these attempts to squelch the Spirit of God working in people's lives, the church flourished. Most stayed true to their faith, despite having their land, houses, possessions, family, freedoms, and lives taken from them. Why? How? Because they had hope. They knew beyond a shadow of a doubt that this world was not the end. As Peter writes, they knew they were "foreigners and exiles" in the world (1 Pet. 2:11). They believed with all their hearts that God had treasures stored up for them in heaven that would far surpass anything here on earth. They knew this because many of them had been eyewitnesses to the life, death, and resurrection of Jesus.

The early Christians saw God's kingdom come in a miraculous way through Jesus. They were taught it had to be lived out in love, compassion, sacrifice, and power. The apostle Paul urged the early church to "Be joyful in hope, patient in affliction, faithful in prayer" (Rom. 12:12) because he knew that "in this hope we were saved. But hope that is seen is no hope at all. Who hopes for what they already have?" (Rom. 8:24). Their momentary struggles could not surpass the eternity of blessings God had stored up for them. We too can have this same attitude, which was the attitude of Christ: "Therefore, since we are surrounded by such a great cloud of witnesses, let us throw off everything that hinders and the sin that so easily entangles. And let us run with perseverance the race marked out for us, fixing our eyes on Jesus, the pioneer and perfecter of faith. For the joy set before him he endured the cross, scorning its shame, and sat down at the right hand of the throne of God" (Heb. 12:2). Jesus knew the suffering he experienced in this world was not the end. He had the joy and hope of heaven. As believers, we have that same hope, but how do we take hold of it during tragic and senseless seasons of our lives?

Primarily, we must be sure to be grounded in our faith. Then, it is imperative that we understand that suffering is like discipline—and discipline is always for our good. Lastly, we have to believe that God's Word is infallible and true.

How do we stay grounded and firm in our faith, and why is this so important? We have all heard of people being drawn closer to God through trials. While this is true, more often than not those people already had a good relationship with the Lord before their challenges began. It is an unfortunate truth that many people with more superficial relationships and no roots lose hope and faith when faced with tragedy.

Let us recall Romans 5:2-5 again: "And we boast in the hope of the glory of God. Not only so, but we also glory in our sufferings, because we know that suffering produces perseverance; perseverance, character; and character, hope. And hope does not put us to shame, because God's love has been poured out into our hearts through the Holy Spirit, who has been given to us." To stay grounded in our faith (which leads to eternal hope), we must remember that God is glorious. We must rejoice in sufferings, and we must allow perseverance and character to be developed in our lives. These things lead to having a hope that does not disappoint.

Rejoicing in Suffering

Rejoicing in the glory of God is the bedrock of solid faith because it keeps us in the right perspective. This attitude of joy in the absolute awesomeness of God helps us see that he is above all and in control of all. Rather than succumbing to a state of disillusionment when things don't go our way and life crumbles around us, it can give us hope that God's mercy, grace, and justice will prevail. Maybe not now, but one day. One day, all things will be made perfect again and will remain so for eternity.

Rejoicing in suffering is also paramount in having a faith that is strong and grounded. This act of the will keeps us from wallowing in self-pity when disaster befalls us. The more we focus on how bad things are, the more we are distracted from God and the more focus we place on ourselves. But if we consider suffering to be joyous, then we can see past the current unpleasantness of our situation and draw encouragement from the promise of our glorious future.

Having a hope that "does not put us to shame" is the end result of allowing perseverance to be carried out in our lives through trials. It is a cornerstone of a rock-solid faith. Where does this hope come from? From Christ alone. The only ultimate hope we have is in the Lord Christ. Our lives may go haywire, but he will always be the same. "A voice says, 'Cry out.' And I said, 'What shall I cry?' 'All people are like grass, and all their faithfulness is like the flowers of the field. The grass withers and the flowers fall, because the breath of the Lord blows on them. Surely the people are grass. The grass withers and the flowers fall, but the word of our God endures forever'" (Isa. 40:6-8).

Continuing on with the perseverance theme, Hebrews 6:11 says, "We want each of you to show this same diligence to the very end, so that what you hope for may be fully realized." God's Holy Spirit, through the author of the book of Hebrews, is encouraging us to stick to our faith, to be grounded and persevere "so that what you hope for may be fully realized." Sticking to our faith makes us secure in our hope, and that very hope can make our faith secure. Hebrews 6:19 notes, "We have this hope as an anchor for the soul, firm and secure. It enters the inner sanctuary behind the curtain."

Our faith must be strong so that we push through adversity, clinging to the hope of God. Our hope in God allows us to push through adversity and retain our faith. Paul reiterates this point in 1 Thessalonians 1:3: "We remember before our God and Father your work produced by faith, your labor prompted by love, and your endurance inspired by hope in our Lord Jesus Christ." Faith and hope work hand-in-hand. Without hope, why have faith? If we have no faith, in what are we to have hope?

Hope is also developed by realizing that our suffering should be considered like discipline. If we are disciplined, then it is always for our good when done by our loving heavenly Father. He loves us and always has our betterment and good in mind.

And have you completely forgotten this word of encouragement that addresses you as a father addresses his son? It says, "My son, do not make light of the

Lord's discipline, and do not lose heart when he rebukes you, because the Lord disciplines the one he loves, and he chastens everyone he accepts as his son." Endure hardship as discipline; God is treating you as his children. For what children are not disciplined by their father? If you are not disciplined—and everyone undergoes discipline—then you are not legitimate, not true sons and daughters at all. Moreover, we have all had human fathers who disciplined us and we respected them for it. How much more should we submit to the Father of our spirits and live! They disciplined us for a little while as they thought best; but God disciplines us for our good, in order that we may share in his holiness. No discipline seems pleasant at the time, but painful. Later on, however, it produces a harvest of righteousness and peace for those who have been trained by it.

—Heb. 12:5-11 NIV

Knowing that the Lord disciplines the ones he loves gives us hope because we realize he is molding us through the difficulties we face. He is still in control and striving to fill us with righteousness and peace through our storms. No matter how bad life is, God is still in control. He will use the mess to make a miracle for those who love him. That is why Paul wrote that "if only for this life we have hope in Christ, we are of all people most to be pitied" (1 Cor. 15:19). The apostle realizes that if we were only looking to the here and now to find our hope (even if that is in our current relationship with Christ), then our lives would be meaningless. Why suffer for the sake of Christ if this is all there is? Why place our trust in the Father if his discipline does not have an eternal outcome?

God's discipline and his allowing pain and suffering to exist in this life can mean horrible things for us temporally, but we have assurance from the Word that our troubles will not be forever. We have a risen Christ who proved that death does not last for those who call him Lord. It is in his promise of eternal salvation that we place our hope and from where our hope springs. Therefore, we can gladly endure hardship because our hope is not in now, but in eternity.

Hope is found and kept when we wholeheartedly believe God's Word is completely true, and when we properly understand his truths. My family used to vacation every year on Hilton Head Island when I was a youth. My brothers and our friends spent hours hanging out at the Shelter Cove Marina. It had shops, restaurants, and huge yachts to ogle.

One day, we heard people chattering around us that John Cougar Mellencamp was down at the marina. We knew there was a small stage where bands would often perform, so we rushed down to the stage to see the free concert. We trusted our sources of information—total strangers—and acted on our trust in their words. To our dismay, upon arriving at the stage, it was empty. No John Cougar. We asked around and found out that he was indeed at the marina, but eating in a restaurant. We had believed the words, and rightly so, but we had not understood the truth of their words. Therefore, our hope (that John Mellencamp was down on stage singing) was false. That left us dejected and accusatory of our information source.

How often does this scenario play out in our lives and the lives of other Christians? We say we believe God's Word, and we act as if we do, but when life turns out other than we think it should, we become suspicious of God and his revealed Word. We think that maybe he wasn't telling the truth after all. "But God's Word says he has 'plans for me, a hope, and a future'. He promised me an 'abundant life.' Where is the good in this disaster?" We've all thought these thoughts. We've all accused God of being false, but he is not. He is love and truth. Jesus said, "I am the way and the truth and the life. No one comes to the Father except through me" (John 14:6). He is truth.

Our problem is that we have been trained to believe the wrong things about God's truths. We have been taught popular opinion about God's Word. Many of us have never sought the Holy Spirit's leading on a passage from the Bible. We have never sought a general consensus from trusted, conservative biblical scholars as to what a passage really means. We read it or hear it in passing and do not take the time to lay hold of the entire picture. This can lead to misery upon misery during or after life's volatile ups and downs.

Pure Spiritual Milk

On the contrary, as Peter exhorts, "Like newborn babies, crave pure spiritual milk, so that by it you may grow up in your salvation" (1 Pet. 2:2). We must starve for the truths and knowledge of God's Word. We must hunger for it, seek it out, and devour it. The psalmist writes, "I have hidden your word in my heart that I might not sin against you" (Ps. 119:11). That is what we must hide in our hearts if we are to survive heartache, loss, tragedy, doubt, fear, and disillusionment.

To have hope, we must have the Word. We must believe the right things about it. We have to ask God to give us faith to believe all Scripture. Not all of it is easy to believe, especially if we do not have a good understanding of it or the context. We must ask the Holy Spirit to guide us into all wisdom and truth. We must ask Jesus to help us with our unbelief. If we do these things and allow God's Spirit to do them in us, then we can be certain that "the God of hope will fill you with all joy and peace as you trust in him, so that you may overflow with hope by the power of the Holy Spirit" (Rom. 15:13).

This raises the question: Where was our hope in the midst of our struggle? Where is your hope for right now? We had just buried our first child; the other two had almost no chance for survival. Where was our hope right then and there? It was in heaven. The only true, lasting, honest hope we had in the midst of tragedy, heartache, and suffering was Christ. Everything else may fade away. Promises by doctors often fall short of the mark. Promises from loved ones may have no merit because they do not hold the keys to the future. The comfort of friends and loved ones certainly carries weight and brings joy, but what if they are not around? What if their words of love and encouragement fail? If we hope in Christ, we will never be disappointed. We may be upset in the way things turn out, but the person and promises of Jesus will always give us hope. Why? Because he is truth. He is risen. He is the Lord and our only true hope now and for the future.

Reflection Questions

1. Where does your hope lie and why?
2. Do you think it is an accurate statement that our only true hope can be in Christ? Why or why not?
3. Where have you turned for hope? People, money, or substances? Have they fulfilled your desire for lasting peace and hope?
4. Do you think you can look to Jesus as your only real source of hope?
5. How can you have hope that God's will is the best when things don't go according to your plan?
6. What were the steps outlined in this chapter to help you have a greater hope in Christ?

Chapter 17

Endurance

He gives strength to the weary and increases
the power of the weak.

—Isa. 40:29

BACK AT THE hospital after Reece's funeral service, we had to change our personas. It was like we couldn't be sad anymore. We had to be strong and upbeat for Sophie and Vivian. We didn't want to emit any negative vibes to the girls. We only wanted to throw off positive emotions in all our thoughts and prayers. It was so hard to be there and try to stay upbeat when we missed Reece so much. We had only buried her minutes ago. The nurses and RTs knew we had just returned from the funeral. Their eyes showed that they hurt for us.

The remainder of that day Ryanne and I stayed glued to our babies' sides. We were no longer guests of the hospital; we would have to go home that evening. We could no longer sleep only moments away from the girls. There would be no more waking at 3:00 AM and walking down to the NICU to check on them. We were fifteen minutes away, much too far if our babies needed us. Most parents don't let their newborns out of their sight for six months to a year. However, we would be leaving our girls at a hospital with people we barely knew, and we would be at home without them. We stretched out that day as long as we could. We didn't want to leave our little angels.

We did not go to church the next day. Instead, we rose early and returned to the hospital to see Sophie and Vivian. We did the same thing the next day. We spent as much time as we could at the NICU. Ryanne wasn't feeling great just yet, so we went home, took an afternoon nap, and ate dinner before going back to the NICU in the evenings.

For some odd reason, I went back to work on Tuesday. I must have felt the need to provide for my family. I reasoned that I would go back then so that I could take two weeks off when Sophie and Vivian came home. Looking back, I wish I had taken one more week off to be with the girls and Ryanne all day, every day. It would have been good to recuperate and get myself back together emotionally instead of going back to seeing patients a mere three days after burying my little Reece. In any event, I went back to work. A basic timeline of life looked like this:

6:00 AM: Wake up
8:00 AM: Arrive at NICU
8:45 AM: Go to work while Ryanne stayed with the girls
1:00 PM: Pick Ryanne up at the NICU; go out for a quick lunch; rush back to the NICU
2:45 PM: Return to work while Ryanne went home to rest
7:00 PM: Leave work; go home; eat dinner; return to NICU
11:00 PM: Leave NICU for the evening; try to sleep, and start over in a few hours

When we were in the NICU, our time consisted of sitting in rocking chairs or stools next to the babies' beds, or simply standing next to them. We liked sitting on the stool. It was tall enough to look over into their beds. The rocking chairs were too short to get a good view. Only a few of the rocking chairs had cushions, so all the parents tried to get those. If we left the NICU—even for a little while—"our" cushioned chair would most likely be occupied when we returned. It was survival of the fittest as far as rocking chairs go—every parent for himself. It seemed like the same for the babies in there too. Which ones would have the capacity to fight it out and live? Which ones would God extend earthly grace to? To which babies would he extend eternal mercy and take home?

Vivian's and Sophia's beds were not directly beside each other. We had to split our time between the two of them. We stayed fifteen minutes at one girl's bed, and then moved to the other baby's bed. Sometimes, Ryanne stayed by one bed and I at the other. Then we switched. We read to the girls and sang to them. Ryanne had purchased each girl her own children's Bible. We kept them by their beds and read stories to them out of it each day.

Ryanne would sing "Jesus Loves Me" and "Mr. Moon." I sang everything under the sun, from Bon Jovi to Stevie Wonder to Elvis. We prayed with them, talked to them, and told them how much we loved them and how strong they were. We told them we would take them to Disneyworld and Hawaii one day. We talked about their home and their family. They probably wished we would be quiet so they could sleep! But we wanted to encourage them 24/7 and let them know we were right there.

When I was at work, I didn't want to be. I had a difficult time being compassionate with my staff or my patients. Anytime I heard someone complain about how bad their back hurt or what awful life event they were faced with, I couldn't help but think, *So you think you've got it bad? Let me tell you about having it bad!*

I felt as if Ryanne and I were on an island by ourselves, separated from the rest of civilization. No one could understand the depths of our anguish. I felt as if no one had life as difficult as we did, and I didn't want to hear about how they thought they did. I now know this is not true. Suffering and anguish can always be put in perspective. Compared to the atrocities of warring factions in Africa, genocide in Eastern Europe, and famine in central Asia, our situation was a cakewalk. But when one is in the middle of the most difficult time in life, it is easy to embrace self pity.

The first full week I was back to work, the girls' status didn't change much. Sophia looked healthier than Vivian. I guess the severity of Vivian's brain bleed made thriving more difficult. We prayed so hard that God would heal her. We continually told Vivian that she was being healed. Everyone would be so amazed when they took her next ultrasound because she would be all better! We prayed the same prayers for Sophia and gave her the same affirmations.

More Bad News

I was with a patient during my second week back to work, when my receptionist paged me. I had a phone call from the NICU. Ryanne and I had developed a system where she would call me on my cell if something bad was happening and I needed to come ASAP. In case I ever received a call like that, I had been parking my car at the edge of our parking lot, facing the street so I could get out quickly. If everything was fine, and Ryanne was just calling to say hello, then she would call the office phone.

When the front desk paged me, I excused myself from my treatment room and stepped over to my private office. Ryanne was not on the other end of the call. It was one of the doctors from the NICU. He had just seen the results from the girls' morning brain ultrasounds. I was excited because I knew he was going to tell me that Vivian's and Sophia's conditions had improved. Instead, he informed me that Sophia's brain hemorrhage had enlarged from a Grade I to a Grade III, and Vivian's condition was still the same—Grade IV, the worst.

My first thought was denial. "Are you sure they didn't get the names wrong on the scans?" I asked.

He was sure. However, I wasn't convinced. I wouldn't be convinced until I saw the images myself. I couldn't understand how this could be. All the prayers we had lifted up for these prognoses to improve couldn't have produced results worse than before. It just wasn't possible! I wouldn't accept it. My faith had to heal my girls. It had to.

"I called you at work because I wanted to tell you as soon as I could," the doctor went on. "I didn't want Ryanne being responsible for relaying the bad news to you when she returned the NICU later."

Ryanne had dropped me off at work that afternoon after lunch, and she had gone home to rest. I called her and asked her to come back and get me so that we could go see the girls. I explained the situation to her over the phone. I was glad it didn't have to be the other way around. Usually, she was at the hospital during this time of day, but that day she went home and took her rest earlier than usual. It was obviously supposed to be that way so she didn't have to receive the bad news by herself and have to call me with the grim report. God always works things out the best for his children. I knew that, but I was having a difficult time believing it. How could worsening brain hemorrhages be good?

Once back at the hospital, Sophia's nurse told me the doctor would come over in a little while to talk to us in person. I was glad to hear that because I still wasn't convinced he had viewed the correct ultrasounds. Sophia couldn't be worse, and Vivian couldn't be the same. This guy must be wrong about their brain imaging results.

When the doctor arrived at Sophia's bedside, he expressed his sorrow for giving us bad news. Then he said, "I'm very surprised to see the results from today's scans. I hadn't expected this to happen. The bleeding in Sophia's lateral ventricles has increased significantly, but not enough to bleed out into the surrounding brain tissue."

This was good news, because if that had occurred, she would most likely have developmental delays, as we expected with Vivian.

"Things could get worse," the doctor told us, "but hopefully they'll remain the same … or even improve."

We had not heard before that things could improve once they were this bad, but he said there was a possibility of remission.

The doctor was not finished. "Sophia has blood clots blocking the cerebrospinal fluid from flowing to its proper destinations. If those clots don't resolve, she could develop swelling in her head known as hydrocephaly. If this happens, Sophia will need some type of external or internal drain to take the excess fluid off her brain."

He went on to explain that excess fluid would lead to excess pressure on the brain. Excess pressure on the brain is a bad thing. It causes all kinds of problems. Now, along with the weekly ultrasounds, the nurses would also be monitoring her head circumference to see if it was swelling.

"I'm also calling in a neurosurgeon to perform another exam on Sophia to determine if any other action needed to be taken immediately," he finished. The neurosurgeon was on vacation and would be back the next week. Obviously, we thought nothing needed to be done very soon, or he would have called in someone currently available.

As upset as we were, at least we had a sliver of hope that there had been complete remissions from Grade II or Grade III bleeds. It meant Sophia at least had a chance. Ryanne and I believed God could even heal Vivian's Grade IV bleed.

After the doctors and nurses left us alone, we held each other and tried to be as encouraging to Sophia as we could. I hated that the doctor stood next to her as he gave us such bad news. I did not like her being exposed to any negativity. So, after the doctor and nurses vacated the area, Ryanne and I told Sophia how great she was doing, and that we loved her, and that God was going to totally heal her, and everything was going to be okay. We wanted to let her know that we believed she was going to be fine and that she needed to believe us and not some ultrasound report. We were just a few days into being parents and we were already trying to shield our kids from the harshness of life. It's funny how we do that. I think there is a lesson to be learned here.

After spending a few more minutes with Sophia, we went over to see Vivian. She was looking good that day. We told her how pretty and sweet she was, and that God was going to heal her too. Maybe their awful condition was just another way for God to show off how he could still perform miracles. Vivian had recently developed an infection and she was on a couple of strong antibiotics to combat it. They told us the medicines should clear the infection quickly. We hoped it would.

Punching and Kicking

Ryanne and I stayed with the girls for the remainder of that afternoon. We sat by them or stood next to them. Sometimes, we put our hands under their warming tents and held their little hands or feet. At times, the girls were very animated, like they were agitated or upset. They would kick and punch, and kick and punch. Then we would put both of our hands under the tent and cup their arms and legs close to their chest. This was supposed to mimic their positions in utero and should calm them down. Sometimes it worked, and sometimes it didn't.

Thinking back to Ryanne's ultrasounds when she was pregnant, none of the girls were ever in that position. They were always sprawled out all over the place. I don't know how that was possible, considering the close quarters they shared, but it seemed to be the case.

Vivian did not respond to the cupping method as well as Sophia did. Vivian preferred to have her little hands touching her face, and she liked to kick one leg out at all times. If Ryanne tried to move her leg back onto the cloth rolled up under her knees, Vivian would immediately kick that leg back out. If we tried to hold her arms down, she would push against our hand until we let go. Then she would start punching and flailing again. She had a lot of fight in her, and she loved to be in motion, just like her daddy. I've got this thing where whenever I'm still, I'm still moving. For example, even as I'm typing, my legs are swaying back and forth, moving in and out as I sit at the desk. Vivian was a chip off the old block.

Sophia was more docile, more like her mama. She liked to kick and punch too, but not as much as Vivian. Sophia would calm down quickly, compared to her sister. Sophia also loved to hold our fingers; Vivian too, but not as often.

Their entire hands wouldn't fit around only half of my pinkie finger. The girls were so tiny that my wedding band fit around their arms all the way up to their shoulders—and I have skinny fingers. One of the sweetest things I ever experienced was when my girls latched onto my finger. They would squeeze it so tight as if to say, "I'm trying so hard, Daddy." I knew they were.

We left the NICU pretty late that St. Patrick's Day night. Ryanne's best friend and Reece's middle namesake, Valerie, was coming in that evening from California with her husband and their little girl. Valerie had been upset for Ryanne and wanted to be near. They were not arriving until midnight, so we stayed up with the girls until it was time to go home and meet Valerie, Dave, and their daughter, Savannah Ryanne.

The next day we noticed that Vivian was lethargic. It was obvious that she didn't feel well due to her infection. Normally, she was little Ms. Active, but that day she just lay around, not moving much. The nurses said the meds had knocked her out and zapped her strength. The doctors continued to suggest we take her off life support. They didn't think there was even a slight possibility her brain would heal. Their position was such that if Vivian's heart and lungs remained strong, then she would survive only as an invalid in a vegetative state. It would be in Vivian's best interest if we let her go. They told us how some parents had opted to not "pull the plug" and how they had come back and told the doctors how they regretted their decision to sustain their child's life because it became so miserable for them to exist as they grew.

Ryanne and I, however, believed that we had to give Vivian the same fighting chance we were giving Sophia. We felt God would not have allowed these girls to be born during a time with all these medical advances if he didn't want us to take advantage of them. Only time would tell if we were right or just selfish. We didn't want to lose another child.

Sophia was doing the same as the day before. She looked good, strong, and healthy. We had a hard time believing she had a severe brain bleed. Another doctor was in that day, and she let me look at the girls' ultrasounds. I wanted to see for myself that it wasn't some type of labeling error, where they copied Sophia's name onto a duplicate copy of Vivian's scan.

Unfortunately, the scans were very different. The images were not the same, and that was deflating. I had hoped the doctors had made an error when reading Sophie's scans. At least I still had the hope that God would heal them both. I knew he could, but even if he chose not to, I knew their future was secure in heaven with him. And I was certain that one day Ryanne and I would be with them.

We planned to go to church on Sunday. It would be our first Sunday back since all this began. We knew it would be tough. Everyone would want to talk to us and hug on us, and we knew that would make us cry. But we felt it was time to go back, and we wanted everyone who knew Ryanne's friend Valerie to see her. Also, I had been thinking about that passage from Reece's funeral, where King David cleaned himself up and went to worship after his baby passed. Ryanne and I wanted and needed to go, but God had other plans.

Chapter 18

How Can You Believe Someone You Can't See and Never Hear From?

T HE NICU WAS always quiet except for the gentle hum and vibrations of the ventilator machines and the soft beeps of the monitoring equipment. The doctors and nurses say the babies have the best opportunity for recovery in a quiet, relaxing environment. That is understandable. Who likes a lot of noise and distraction when they are sick?

Ryanne and I never digested the memo about keeping quiet. We talked to our girls all the time. It was our opinion they needed to know that we were there. We wanted to give them constant encouragement. We felt they wanted to hear our voices, to listen to Mommy and Daddy speak words of praise and love. Apparently, according to the doctors, they would rather hear nothing but the sound of silence.

We believed that hearing from us had to be better than not hearing from us. Had we crept into the NICU and never made our presence known, would the girls have wondered where we were? Had we merely sat beside them in complete silence, would they have thought Mommy and Daddy had abandoned them? Would they have felt neglected and alone?

Would they have felt loved? Was it possible they would have wondered if their parents even existed? We didn't like these options, so we communicated. We communicated a lot. Sometimes we talked to them. Other times we read to them or sang to them. We prayed for them often. We wanted them to know we were there. That is the only way we could help them … just by being there.

Communication is Key

Through all of this, our thoughts turned to our relationship with God. Ryanne and I began searching our hearts and wondering how often had we accused God of not being present, or hearing us, or answering our prayers because we didn't hear an audible voice from him. Could it be that even though we often did not feel or hear God's presence during those dark days that he actually was still present? Though we did not feel him present, was he still seated on his kingdom throne? We thought so, but we were not convinced. Everything we had ever thought or been taught about God's love, caring nature, attentiveness to detail in our lives, and trustworthiness was coming into question. How could we trust God with anything when he seemed to be so apathetic to this great struggle? If he is there, doesn't he care? Those questions burned at the core of our beings as we tried to hang on to our faith.

Communication is key in any relationship. Since we weren't hearing any communication orally, the Bible is what kept us locked into our faith in God. His Word held the direct rebuttal to each and every doubt mentioned above. Without our history of knowing, reading, and studying God's Word, such a time as this would have been impossible. Finding Scripture to apply to our questions and doubts would have been much more difficult had many of their truths not been hidden in our hearts.

Thousands of years ago, God communicated his truths to humanity through Scripture. He tells us plainly that if we want to know him we need to know his Word. Second Timothy 3:16 reads, "All Scripture is God-breathed and is useful for teaching, rebuking, correcting and training in righteousness." God impressed upon the hearts and minds of men what to write and how to write it. Hence the term *God-breathed.* Another thing in this verse is that when we experience doubt, discouragement, despair, or whatever the case may be, God's holy Word can teach us the truth, rebuke the lies in our hearts and heads, correct our wrong thinking, and build us up in the likeness of God. This is so important when we are in the midst of, as Zig Ziglar calls it, episodes of "stinking thinking." When we don't know what to think about our lives, or God's involvement in our lives, we can turn to the Word to get our hearts and minds set in the right direction again. Can friends help? Sometimes. Can books like this one help? Hopefully. But our real hope is found in the Word, where God is forever speaking. "The grass withers and the flowers fall, but the word of our God endures forever" (Isa. 40:8).

> Now, Israel, hear the decrees and laws I am about to teach you. Follow them so that you may live and may go in and take possession of the land the Lord, the God of your ancestors, is giving you. Do not add to what I command you and do not subtract from it, but keep the commands of the Lord your God that I give you.
>
> —Deut. 4:1-2

It is our responsibility and privilege to know and obey God's Word ("decrees," "laws," "commands"). Why?

Because this Word is God's primary tool of communication with his creation. His Word is what makes it possible to go and take possession of the land. It gives us life. As Ryanne and I sat in the NICU rocking chairs beside our girls, doubts and fears strangled life from our hopes and beliefs. In your life, lies, unbelief, and misunderstanding of God and what his Word says can and will do the same. When our minds were filled with anything other than the truths of God's Word, we did not walk in victory through our battles, and neither can you. We must know his Word and live by it.

Being Sanctified by the Holy Spirit

In the gospel of John, Jesus prays for his disciples when he asks God to "Sanctify them by the truth; your word is the truth. As you sent me into the world, I have sent them into the world. For them I sanctify myself, that they too may be truly sanctified" (John 17:17-19). This Scripture tells us plainly that Jesus' desire is for his believers to be sanctified—set apart by God's truth—which is his Word. He then goes on to proclaim he is setting himself apart so that the disciples may attain true sanctification.

Jesus is God's Word, as we have established above. He is truth. He is the sanctification. He is the standard by which all truth is based. He is the pinnacle of what we aspire to when we desire to be set apart for God's call and purpose. Considering all this, how can that apply when a loved one lies dying or when you have just been handed a pink slip and don't know from where your next paycheck is coming? It is simply this realization: Jesus is the answer to the madness. He is the truth beyond the lies of death, sickness, poverty, discouragement, and doubt that we face. He is different from the world. He is sanctified, set apart. How? Because he is God. Also, because he willingly gave himself up to die on the cross. He set himself apart to receive the condemnation that we all deserved, so that we could be set apart as his children now and forever.

Owning this truth, this information, can block any fiery darts Satan may throw our way in the form of tragedy, heartache, or loss. When we are in Christ, when we are his disciples, we are different because of his Word living in us. And we have the capability to call upon that power at all times.

Such power is displayed in John 1:1-2, which states that "In the beginning was the Word, and the Word was with God, and the Word was God. He was with God in the beginning." Here we see two truths: Jesus is God and Jesus is the Word. If Jesus is a direct representation of who God is to humankind (nature, power, love, grace, mercy, justice), then God's Word is a direct representation of himself as well. This verse has huge ramifications whenever one doubts God's love, presence, or caring. Why? Because Scripture paints the perfect portrait of God. We just have to know the painting to grasp the power. At our fingertips, through Scripture, we have the power and presence of the one and only, almighty God.

As long as we peer into the vivid landscape of God's masterpiece, then we can have at our disposal all the riches of his grace when we need them. I am referring to Scripture memorization. It is only through years of study that an art major can look at a painting and tell you the artist, year, motif, and motivation behind an adorned canvas. How much more attention should we give to the unsearchable mind of God regarding his Word? How much more will it benefit us during hardships to know what God has said over the eons, rather than what the world says at the present?

Not only do we need to be able recall the power of God's Word through our memory, but we also need to be sure we properly understand how to apply it to our lives at a given time. A gallery owner or curator cannot phone Van Gogh and ask him for his interpretation of *Starry Night*. But through the Holy Spirit who lives in us, we as believers have direct access to the Painter for his interpretation of his work. For someone who does not have a personal relationship with Christ, the Bible is a greater mystery than to a believer. This is because the Bible is clear that only those who have a belief and faith in Jesus Christ as Lord and Savior get the full benefit of the Holy Spirit living in them. For example: "And I will ask the Father, and he will give you another advocate to help you and be with you forever—the Spirit of truth. The world cannot accept him, because it neither sees him nor knows him. But you know him, for he lives with you and will be in you" (John 14:16-17).

Thankfully, the Spirit of God still works on hearts and minds, as he has done with countless persons who have come to faith in Christ. John 16:8 tells us that "When he comes, he will prove the world to be in the wrong about sin and righteousness and judgment." This assures us that God's Spirit is forever calling us to him. This is true even before we know Christ. That is why someone who is not a disciple of Jesus can still grasp some parts of Scripture, particularly parts leading to that person giving his or her life to Christ. On the other hand, those who have no belief and faith in Jesus Christ, and do not have the benefit of the Holy Spirit living in them, often pull a Scripture out of the hat and condemn God. They say he does not exist, or that he is a liar, or some other thing, showing they have no hold on what the Bible teaches. They don't have the Holy Spirit guiding them in their understanding and interpretation of Scripture.

Believers have the full benefit of the Holy Spirit to apply, understand, comprehend, and interpret Scripture. We need to take advantage of this gift. Throughout the ordeal with our girls, Ryanne and I had many conversations with Christians trying to comfort us with God's Word. But they dropped verses out of context or used Scripture with their own faulty interpretations. Just because a house has a dishwasher doesn't mean the owner will use it every time. This, unfortunately, is how a lot of Christians (myself included) approach the Counselor or Advocate. Jesus called the Holy Spirit the Advocate: "And I will ask the Father, and he will give you another advocate to help you and be with you forever" (John 14:16). "But the Advocate, the Holy Spirit, whom the Father will send in my name, will teach you all things and will remind you of everything I have said to you" (John 14:26). He is called the Advocate for good reason. He is like a lawyer for believers. Just as we would hire an attorney to go over a lease agreement and interpret words, phrases, and paragraphs we did not understand, the Holy Spirit can do the same for us with God's Word.

Not only does the Holy Spirit help us navigate God's Word and apply it properly to our lives by being our Counselor or Advocate, he is also our power (Luke 24:49) and our direct revelation from God about his plans for our lives (1 Cor. 2:9-10). He is the revealer of the mind of God (1 Cor. 2:11) and of all spiritual truths (1 Cor. 2:13). He gives us the ability to accept the things of God (1 Cor. 2:14), and he is the presence of God's love poured out in our lives (Rom. 5:5).

God uses his Holy Spirit living in us to show us so many things, but primarily he uses the Holy Spirit to show us that he is there, he is real, and that he loves us.

Prayer

God speaks to us through his Word and his Spirit. He also communicates with us through prayer.

In 1 Thessalonians 5:17, the apostle Paul instructs believers to "pray continually." If Paul, through the prompting of God's Holy Spirit, thought it important enough to tell the church at Thessalonica to always pray, shouldn't believers everywhere take his command just as seriously today? Paul realized that prayer is a key to believers maintaining a relationship with God. If someone went for days or weeks without speaking to their spouse, would the relationship flourish? Would the husband know the wife's needs? Would the wife understand her husband's concerns? Of course not. This is why God instituted prayer. Prayer gives people a direct line of communication with heaven. Prayer is how we speak to him. Meditation is when God speaks to us as we listen. Communication is a two-way street. It is not enough to simply get on our knees and lay out our laundry list of wants to God and then get up and go on with our busy lives.

To truly hear from God, we must slow down and allow for some time to hear. God will speak through his Spirit directly to our hearts, but he will also speak through his Spirit directly through the Word. Taking time to reflect and listen is crucial to our communication with God. He does speak; we just have to listen. If we don't listen, we end up missing God's part of the conversation. Missing what he has to say leads to a lot of heartache and misunderstanding. How many times have I thought one thing to be true about the Word or life or God only to find out the hard way I was wrong? The answer is many. If I had taken time to hear from God about what his Word really meant on one thing or another, I would not have had such a difficult learning curve.

Do Not Be Anxious

I believe that one of the greatest set of verses in the Bible on prayer and communication is found in the apostle Paul's letter to the Philippians: "Do not be anxious about anything, but in every situation, by prayer and petition, with thanksgiving, present your requests to God. And the peace of God, which transcends all understanding, will guard your hearts and your minds in Christ Jesus" (Phil 4:6-7). Why are these two verses so great? There are two reasons.

The first reason is that we are instructed to not worry about anything. "Do not be anxious about anything." How often do we worry instead of pray? How often do we pray and still worry? Being anxious after we pray about something really shows no faith on our part. It's like saying to God that we are going to give him this dilemma, sickness, or concern to take care of—but not really. We're not going to entrust it to him entirely. We're still going to worry about it. How much sense does that make? Yet, think of how often we do that. Instead of giving our requests to God with thanksgiving and expecting him to handle them, we give him our requests half-heartedly and then hang on to the anxiety that he probably won't come through.

When we forgo the anxiety after prayer, everything is changed. We are freed from the shackles of doubt and worry, and a weight is immediately lifted. This happens when believers go to prayer with an attitude of thanks. This is why Paul can write about the peace of God transcending all understanding and guarding our hearts and minds in Christ Jesus. Our hearts and minds can and will be guarded in that peace and comfort that no one can understand when we fully give our lives-including all our requests, concerns, and worries-over to God through prayer. We communicate our fears and needs to him; he communicates his love and peace to us. He not only communicates it to us, but he also freely gives it to us and builds a wall of protection around our hearts and minds with it. God wants to give us understanding and protection. It is amazing how much he loves us.

We Must Invite Him In

Though he is not physically present in our lives on a daily basis, we can trust God and put our faith in him. We can trust him because he tells us we can. He tells us this through his Word. The Bible is God's way of communicating eternal truths to us. It is one of his ways to show us he is real and present. It is a means to convey his love for us and that he has our best interests at heart all the time.

Though God has set up his Word, the Holy Spirit, and prayer to usher us into a trusting relationship, it is up to us to actively seek out that relationship. It is our responsibility to spend time in prayer, to read and study Scripture, and to fellowship with other believers in the Holy Spirit. Our relationship with God is just that—a relationship. This implies that two parties are actively involved. God is a gentleman, and he will not force his way into our lives. We must invite him in. He gives us the choice to get to know him or not. We need to cultivate our relationship with God through the ways discussed above. When we do, we will find he is completely worthy of all of our trust and praise.

Reflection Questions

1. What are the primary ways mentioned in this chapter that we can learn of God's love and trustworthiness?
2. Though you may have gone through a situation (or are in the middle of one) that makes you question God's

love and trustworthiness, how do you now know he really has your best interests at heart?

3. Is it necessary to fully understand God and his plans to trust him? Why or why not?

4. What steps will you take to develop a stronger, more personal relationship with the God who loves you?

Chapter 19

Fighter

Give thanks to the Lord, for he is good.
His love endures forever.

—Ps. 136:1

SUNDAY MORNING THE phone rang at 7:45 AM. It was
Christina, one of the nurses from the NICU. When you
get a phone call at an odd hour from the NICU, your heart
drops to your knees.

"Vivian has just experienced a couple of episodes, where
her heart rate dropped significantly," the nurse said. "She's
stable right now. I wanted to let you know what happened.
There's no immediate rush, but you might want to come
up here."

Ryanne and I quickly got ready, told Valerie what was
going on, and rushed to the hospital. I was scheduled to
teach the youth Sunday school class that morning, so I called
our youth minister and told him I wouldn't be able to make
it. When we arrived at the hospital, we were surprised and
encouraged to see him waiting for us.

"I wanted to come by and see if there's anything I can do for you," Brett said.

"Please have everyone pray for Vivian," we pleaded. As Brett headed back to church, Ryanne and I went into the NICU to see our little girls.

Once at Vivian's side, Christina came over and gave us more details about what had happened. Vivian was doing fine when she arrived that morning at 6:45 AM. Then at 7:15 AM, her heart rate suddenly dropped from the mid-hundreds to seventy-something. They gave her two shots of epinephrine directly into her heart, performed manual respiration with the bag, and did chest compressions. It was like Day One all over again!

Over the phone Christina had made it sound like it was no big deal, but hearing it from her now sounded like a *very* big deal. I should have known something bad had happened for her to call when she did. We had seen the girls' heart rates drop on several occasions, from the mid-hundreds to the nineties or upper-eighties. A few seconds of tickling their backs or feet would always bring their heart rates back up. That scenario played out daily, but this situation was not like those times. With such a dramatic drop in heart rate, Vivian had almost died … again.

The doctor came over and related the same episode. He also told us that Vivian's most recent blood test looked worse instead of better. Due to the heavy antibiotics they had been administering, she had developed a serious yeast infection. Antibiotics not only kill bad bacteria, but they also kill good bacteria, like the ones that keep yeast cultures at bay. The yeast had proliferated rapidly and invaded Vivian's entire body.

This was bad. Yeast uses oxygen to thrive and reproduce. It can happen to anyone who takes antibiotics, but it was adversely affecting Vivian more than normal because of her compromised condition. The doctors were doing all they could, but most likely this morning was a prelude of things to come. The infection would continue to feed off Vivian's oxygen, taking from her what she needed to survive. This would cause her muscles to lose their ability to function properly. Since her heart was a muscle, it meant her heart rate would continue to drop until it became pointless to try further resuscitation. Basically, her heart would fatigue due to lack of oxygen, and she would pass away.

"Would you like to go ahead and declare her a Do Not Resuscitate?" the doctor asked.

"We're not willing to make that call just yet," I told him.

Unless you've had a medical professional give your baby a zero percent chance of survival, you can't imagine the depth of grief that overtakes you. I suppose the only scenario that comes close is getting the same prognosis about a spouse or a close family member. We knew Vivian had been facing an uphill battle since she was born. The problems she had on her birthday and the development of her brain bleed didn't help matters. However, Ryanne and I had been holding out hope that although things didn't look good for her, she would still get better. We had prepared for the worst to come at any time over that past three weeks, but we didn't want to believe it would really happen.

We prayed so hard over little Vivian those next few moments. We told her how strong she was and how much better she was going to be. We believed that God would miraculously bring her through this infection. Even with our exercise of faith we could not help but see that Vivian was definitely weaker now. She was no longer as animated as she had been even a few days before. She just lay on her back, motionless. That was definitely not normal for her.

Although we had received such bad news, we could still experience joy in our precious daughter. She was the sweetest thing. That day her left eye was closed, but her right eye was partially open. Her ventilator tube was pulling her lip up and to the right. She looked like she was doing an Elvis impersonation. It was so cute.

That Sunday we spent the majority of our day with Vivian. Poor little Sophie didn't get much attention, but we explained to her the reason why. The nurses allowed Ryanne to hold Vivian. We appreciated that, but it was hard to hear the nurse's reason: "We figured we might as well let you, because it can't do her any more harm."

Nevertheless, Ryanne was elated to hold her baby. We pulled up a chair close to Vivian's bed. The nurses wrapped Vivian in some blankets and gave her IVs and tubes some slack. Then they picked her up and handed her to Ryanne.

As Ryanne held little Vivian, we smiled through tears of happiness and sorrow. Our sweet little Vivian was so tough, and so strong, and she was fighting so hard. We were proud of our daughter and how determined she was. But we were so scared we would soon lose her. We didn't want her to go on living if she was going to suffer now or in the future, but we didn't want her to die either. Our only desire was that God heal all that was wrong with Vivian, and we had come to the realization that he may choose to heal her in heaven.

Ryanne had expressed to me during the drive to the hospital that morning that she could not handle the loss of another baby. Yet, here she was, going through what appeared to be the end of our time with our second child. Ryanne is so strong. She is such a great mother, too. I know Vivian could sense the love and strength of her mother. Just being next to those two pillars of determination was such an amazing experience for me. I have never seen two women so completely dedicated to life and to each other. My admiration for my wife and my daughter grew by leaps and bounds that day. Sophia was equally inspiring. She spent most of the day by herself, toughing it out, so that her mom and I could spend time with Vivian, her little sick sister.

Ryanne asked if I wanted to hold Vivian. I did so badly, but I didn't want Ryanne to have to give her up. So, I just let her hold Vivian. Ryanne held the baby and I kneeled beside Ryanne and held both of them. It was a special and wonderful time that I'll never forget. How I wish it could have gone on forever, and that we could have taken turns holding all of our little girls in their peak of health.

Ryanne and I stayed in the NICU all day. We didn't want to leave Vivian's side for one moment because we didn't know when it could be her last. Though she had been stable all day, her heart rate had been dropping little by little throughout the day. It should have been in the 140s to the 150s, but it was only in the 110s now. That night the transition room was available, so we stayed in the NICU by Vivian's side. Valerie brought us an overnight bag from home. My parents brought up dinner from Outback. We all ate in the second floor waiting room. We were sitting out in the labor and delivery waiting area, not in anticipation of our child being born like all other families, but expecting that one of our children was about to die.

Ryanne and I had a good night with the girls. We slept very little—just naps here and there—but we slept well when we did sleep. I awoke at 4:30 AM and went out to check on the babies. One of the nurses from our first night in the hospital was hanging out in the NICU that night. Her aunt had been my patient.

About two minutes after I returned to the transition room from checking on the girls, and just as I was getting back into bed, *bang, bang, bang.* Three loud knocks on the door sent our hearts racing. I jumped up and rushed to the door, fearing the worst. How could anything bad have happened in the few seconds I had been away? It was the nurse I just mentioned. She had a couple of boxes of cereal and some juice for us. A nice gesture, but a little ill-timed. She scared us to death. Ryanne and I got back into bed and slept for another couple hours after our hearts stopped beating out of our chests.

Vivian's Heart Rate Drops Even More

When we woke, we checked on the babies first thing. Sophia was doing well, really holding her own. Vivian's condition had not changed. Her heart rate was still in the 110s. We took showers, put on clean clothes, and immediately went back out to the girl's bedsides. After sitting with Vivian for about forty-five minutes with her condition unchanged, I decided I was ready for some of that cereal that was delivered at 4:30 AM! We couldn't have food in the NICU, so I went back to our room and ate breakfast while Ryanne stayed with baby Vivian.

After eating I got down on my knees and begged God for a miracle. We had already lost one precious angel, and I pleaded with him not to take another. After praying, I felt somewhat confident that things were going to be better with Vivian. I had a strange peace that she was going to be healed here on earth.

I walked back out to her bedside. The expression on Ryanne's face let me know that my premonition of Vivian's earthly healing only moments before was off the mark. Ryanne wore a look of terror, grief, and pain. She nodded towards the machine monitoring Vivian's heat rate. It was in the nineties. She had been slowly dropping since I went back for breakfast.

The doctor came over and asked if we had made any decision about the Do Not Resuscitate orders. I informed her that Ryanne and I decided that if resuscitation was needed, we only wanted them to do chest compressions. We didn't want her to have epinephrine injections into her heart again. She still had the two puncture holes from her episode the previous day. We now realized that epinephrine would only prolong her death rather than sustain her life.

Telling the doctor to avoid every avenue possible to save our baby was miserable, but we knew it was the best decision for our daughter. She did not deserve to suffer through another resuscitation effort. If God wanted her in heaven, far be it from us to selfishly try and keep her here in such a miserable state of existence for a few more hours. We realized the end was near for Vivian. We had prayed for her before she was born. When she was born too early, we prayed for her to live despite the odds. When they told us she had an incurable brain condition, we prayed that God would heal her. Now, we prayed that if the Lord chose not to completely heal her here that he would take her and spare her the agony of a completely untenable existence. When any loved one has been diagnosed with a mind-boggling, incurable disease, and their condition quickly transitions from bad to worse, we want comfort and restoration for that loved one when it is obvious an earthly healing is not going to take place.

As Vivian's heart rate continued to drop, our hearts continued to sink. We held each other. We held Vivian's hands. We cried. We told her how much we loved her and how proud of her we were. She was such a strong and pretty little girl.

Once Vivian's heart rate dropped into the seventies (her oxygen concentration levels were now in the fifties instead of near one hundred), the doctor came over and informed us that it was time to start chest compressions. Any sustained time for a baby this tiny below eighty beats per minute would not allow for survival. Proper oxygen would not get to her brain or other tissues.

They unhooked Vivian from the ventilator and used the hand-held ventilator to continue breathing for her. We watched as the nurses, RTs, and the doctor performed CPR on our three-week-old daughter. It was much the same scene we'd witnessed a few weeks earlier with Reece. This time, however, was not so shocking.

When Vivian had gone through resuscitation the first time, we were totally unprepared for it. Now, although we had believed God was going to make her well, we had been preparing for this moment for the past several days. She was severely premature and deathly sick. We knew this, and our intellect did not allow our faith to claim what was insupportable by evidence. Our positive thinking could not get past the harshness of reality. Anyone who has had a terminally ill loved one can relate to the feelings we experienced. We wanted to believe that Vivian would be healed, but deep down we knew it was unlikely, at least not on this side of heaven. We certainly didn't like it, but we accepted it because it seemed as if her end was on the horizon. We began praying for spiritual healing as well as physical healing. We asked God to take care of our sweet, little Vivian in heaven. We asked God to take her home if he had chosen not to heal her here. We wanted what was best for Vivian. If that meant she would be healed only by going to heaven, then we were prepared to accept that scenario. We would bow to God's perfect will so that out daughter could be made instantly perfect.

We tried to be strong for little Vivian. After a few minutes with no increase in her heart rate or oxygen saturation, the doctor asked us what we wanted to do. She said she could do the epinephrine, or they could stop and let us hold her until she passed. As horrifying as it was to agree to, we knew that holding Vivian was the correct decision. We felt like we were giving up on her. At the same time, we felt like we were giving her the opportunity to leave this unwholesome world for the glory of heaven and the companionship of her older sister.

Ryanne got comfortable sitting on a stool beside Vivian's bed. The nurses wrapped Vivian in some blankets and handed her to Ryanne. I kneeled down beside them, and as Ryanne held the baby, I held my wife. We rocked little Vivian for the longest time. I played with Vivian's strawberry blonde hair and kissed her on the forehead. We cried. Then we sobbed. We were so devastated. We were losing our second child. Through tears, Ryanne repeated a phrase that had become all too familiar and all too true, "This is just terrible, so terrible."

This sentence had come to define our lives.

Chapter 20

His Ways Are Not Our Ways

SINCE COMMITTING OUR lives to Jesus, we had given everything to God and tried to live according to his will. We had both been leaders in the youth group at church, stayed away from alcohol and drugs, had consistent quiet times, tried to be kind, loving, and respectful to our parents and peers, waited until we were married to have sex, and generally tried to live a healthy Christian life. Naturally, we failed miserably and deliberately at times, but we always asked for forgiveness and turned back to Christ. Now, we felt as if those periods of sin and disobedience were bringing God's judgment, silence, and apparent dismissal of our current prayers for our girls.

Initially, we thought God allowed Ryanne to go into early delivery so he could miraculously heal the babies and get them out of the NICU. If using that scary situation brought him glory, then we were willing to allow for the temporary pain and suffering. It soon became crystal clear that our understanding of the divine will was way off the mark. Reece was dead. Vivian was dying. We were wrong.

The agony of holding our dying child was compounded by the feeling of God's abandonment in the situation. *Terrible* was the best way to describe everything we felt. Where was God? Why hadn't he heard us and responded? Why didn't he do what we asked him to do? Had we not been faithful to him for all those years? Why was he not being faithful to us now? These questions bombarded our minds and tormented our souls.

Maybe for a second we experienced a tiny fraction of Jesus' suffering as he hung on the cross, bearing the sin, shame, and punishment of the world while he was being forsaken by his Father. God turned his back on his only Son so his holy wrath could be poured out to atone for the sins of humanity. Think of the loneliness Jesus must have felt as he hung there, dying. All of his friends, save a few, had abandoned him and run off into hiding. The people he came to rescue, the Jewish nation, plotted to have him killed. Now, his own heavenly Father would have nothing to do with him in the midst of his darkest hour.

Why did God turn his back on his only Son? Why did Jesus cry out from the cross, "*Eloi, Eloi, lama sabachthani?* (My God, my God, why have you forsaken me?)" (Mark 15:34). Why couldn't God have eradicated sin some other way? Why did Jesus have to die? Why does God allow bad things to happen to us? Why do we have to suffer? Why doesn't he right all wrongs? And why doesn't he do it immediately?

The simple answer is that there is no simple answer. We are told by God communicating through the prophet Isaiah that "'my thoughts are not your thoughts, neither are your ways my ways,' declares the Lord" (Isa. 55:8). This verse tells us that we will never fully know the answers to some of our hardest questions about life and death. We are not on the same level with God. He is great, but we are small. He is mighty, but we are weak. He is all powerful, and we are not even close. We can't comprehend his ways and his thoughts, so when something goes haywire in our lives, there is no way we can possibly grasp the method and reasoning behind the madness. We need to accept this truth.

God Is Awesome

Psalm 8:3-4 reads, "When I consider your heavens, the work of your fingers, the moon and the stars, which you have set in place, what is mankind that you are mindful of them, human beings that you care for them?" What a fitting soliloquy to the awesomeness of God and the mortality of humans. When I read Lee Strobel's book, *The Case for a Creator,* I could not comprehend half of what I read, due to the scientific nature of the discussions he recounted with some of the most brilliant minds in physics and astronomy. If I could not keep up with the dialogue between men, why should I think I could comprehend the mind of Almighty God—the God who gave those men their minds and who created everything they discussed? Knowing next to nothing as I do, why do I feel that I have the right to question God's plan?

When I stop and think about it, it makes no sense. His ways are not our ways. His thoughts are not our thoughts. Psalm 95:3-4 is absolutely correct: "For the Lord is the great God, the great King above all gods. In his hand are the depths of the earth, and the mountain peaks belong to him." What more is there to say about his greatness?

If God is great, mighty, and elevated, where does that leave us? Where does that leave us when we realize we are the clay, and we can't question the potter? We still hurt when we lose loved ones. We still have to endure physical, mental, and emotional pain that we don't like and don't understand. Our lives still contain a lot of junk we wish were not there. Why doesn't God lay out the red carpet for us and all of his followers? Why do we have to suffer as children of the King?

Here is where we have to exercise the trust we discussed in an earlier chapter. We must have faith in God that since he is so great and we are so small, those ways that are not our ways are really and truly for our best interest, even when his plans involve our suffering. This trust is difficult to come by when your beloved spouse or child is dying and you can't do anything to heal them—and God doesn't seem to be intervening on their behalf. Most scholars believe Jesus yelled out the phrase mentioned above (*Eloi, Eloi, lama sabachthani?*) as he was nearing his last breaths on the cross not because he was lashing out at God or questioning him. Rather, it is thought that Jesus was quoting Scripture that prophesied about himself. Jewish boys and girls memorized Scripture pertaining to the coming Messiah. Jesus certainly fit the mold. After all, he was a Jewish boy before he became a Jewish man. The verses he quoted are found in Psalm 22:

> My God, my God, why have you forsaken me? Why are you so far from saving me, so far from my cries of anguish? My God, I cry out by day, but you do not answer, by night, but I find no rest. Yet you are enthroned as the Holy One; you are the one Israel praises. In you our ancestors put their trust; they trusted and you delivered them. To you they cried out and were saved; in you they trusted and were not put to shame. But I am a worm and not a man, scorned by everyone, despised by the people. All who see me mock me; they hurl insults, shaking their heads. "He trusts in the Lord," they say, "let the Lord rescue him. Let him deliver him, since he delights in him." Yet you brought me out of the womb; you made me trust in you, even at my mother's breast. From birth

I was cast on you; from my mother's womb you have been my God. Do not be far from me, for trouble is near and there is no one to help. Many bulls surround me; strong bulls of Bashan encircle me. Roaring lions that tear their prey open their mouths wide against me. I am poured out like water, and all my bones are out of joint. My heart has turned to wax; it has melted within me. My mouth is dried up like a potsherd, and my tongue sticks to the roof of my mouth; you lay me in the dust of death. Dogs surround me, a pack of villains encircles me; they pierce my hands and my feet. All my bones are on display; people stare and gloat over me. They divide my clothes among them and cast lots for my garment. But you, Lord, do not be far from me. You are my strength; come quickly to help me. Deliver me from the sword, my precious life from the power of the dogs. Rescue me from the mouth of the lions; save me from the horns of the wild oxen. I will declare your name to my people; in the assembly I will praise you. You who fear the Lord, praise him! All you descendants of Jacob, honor him! Revere him, all you descendants of Israel! For he has not despised or scorned the suffering of the afflicted one; he has not hidden his face from him but has listened to his cry for help. From you comes the theme of my praise in the great assembly; before those who fear you I will fulfill my vows. The poor will eat and be satisfied; those who seek the Lord will praise him—may your hearts live forever! All the ends of the earth will remember and turn to the Lord, and all the families of the nations will bow down before him, for dominion belongs to the Lord and he rules over the nations. All the rich of the earth will feast and worship; all who go down to the dust will kneel before him—those who cannot keep themselves alive. Posterity will serve him; future generations will be told about the Lord. They will proclaim his righteousness, declaring to a people yet unborn: He has done it!

This psalm gives insight into the mind of Christ and the attitude we should adopt as we endure trials of many kinds. It allows us to understand the trust we should have in the ways and plans of our Creator. The psalmist David wrote this as he was being persecuted and attacked. He was righteous, "a man after God's own heart." Yet, he was in the middle of the valley of the shadow of death. His son and others were trying to take his life. In his distress he initially calls out to God, questioning his lack of intervention in the madness surrounding him. But later we see David's realization that God will not be silent forever in the matter, and that he will rescue and save. This warrants praise from David because he sees the end of the tunnel.

Making It Out of the Valley

David knows that he will walk through the valley and make it out safely on the other side. As believers, we have the same hope, promise, and assurance. Even if the other side of the valley is the other side of eternity, we will make it because God is our strength, shield, protector, defender, and Savior. Therefore, we can have full confidence that God's plans can be trusted. They will all end positively for us. David knew this. Jesus knew it, too. That is why the apostle Paul writes in Philippians 2:8-9 that Jesus, "being found in appearance as a man ... humbled himself by becoming obedient to death—even death on a cross! Therefore God exalted him to the highest place and gave him the name that is above every name." God's plan was greater than the miserable circumstance in which he was involved.

So why do we have to go through the tough times to learn our lessons? Is it just so that God can show his dominion, power, and authority to us? Is it so he can put us in our place? I don't think so. Proverbs 3:11-12 tells why.

The verses are written by King Solomon to his son. The wise king realized that his son would have the same questions we have in relation to the seemingly inexplicable nature of suffering, difficulty, and hardships. That is why he writes, "My son, do not despise the Lord's discipline and do not resent his rebuke, because the Lord disciplines those he loves, as a father the son he delights in."

Solomon thought his son might see strain in his life as if it were some harsh punishment by God. He realized that his child may get angry with God and with the proverbial "cards" he had been dealt at certain times of his life. Solomon understood that his son could misunderstand trials and troubles and get bitter instead of better. Therefore, the Holy Spirit prompts him to write these words of wisdom. He wants his son to have the knowledge beforehand that he will most certainly face the Lord's discipline and rebuke, but that they are for his own good, not his harm. Just as Solomon disciplined and rebuked his own son for his benefit, God would most assuredly do the same. Why? Because he loves us and delights in us. God does not want to see us, his precious children, suffer unnecessarily. When we face challenges, he wants us to learn from them.

A good parent does not correct their child simply for love of disciplining. It is done with a purpose in mind. For example, if a child is shoving too much food in her mouth, the parent will rebuke the child and instruct her to take smaller bites. If she doesn't obey, the parent may take away the plate of food away in order to cut it into smaller bites. The child may get upset because the parent took away the food, but the parent knows the reason. The parent is willing to allow the child to "suffer" for a few seconds because he is acting for the well-being of the child, to protect and instruct. The parent loves the child and wants to make sure she doesn't choke, that she learns proper manners, and that she digests her food well. In short, the parent loves the daughter. That is why he acts. He cannot simply stand by, uninvolved, and allow his child to consistently behave in a manner that is dangerous and unproductive. He wants the best for his child, just as God wants the best for us. Therefore, we may face the refiner's fire, but we must realize there is always a great and noble purpose behind it, a purpose for our improvement because God loves us and cares for us.

Let us walk with confidence through the fire with full faith that God will see us through. His ways are not ours, but because he is greater, his ways are too.

Reflection Questions

1. When or how have you ever felt abandoned by God?
2. How did God assure you that you were not really abandoned? Or have you sensed that assurance yet?
3. From a Christian perspective, is there always a positive end to going through pain, suffering, and trials?
4. What did you learn from this chapter to help you understand why God allows pain and suffering in the lives of believers?
5. How can you use what you have learned to encourage others?

Chapter 21

Sorrow and Pain

Brothers and sisters, we do not want you to be
uninformed about those who sleep in death,
so that you do not grieve like the rest of
mankind, who have no hope.
—1 Thess. 4:13

V IVIAN'S MONITORS HAD been cut off when she was
handed to Ryanne. After several minutes of being alone
with her, the doctor came over and checked Vivian's heart
and breath sounds. She dropped her head, looked at us, and
told us that she was sorry, but Vivian was gone.

For the second time in three weeks, we heard the awful
pronouncement of death for one of our children. That is
not something you ever want to hear once, much less twice.
The doctor told us we could hold her as long as we wanted.
They would clean her up and take all her tubes and lines
out after we were done. Then, if we wanted, we could hold
her in the transition room for a little while longer.

After holding Vivian and praying that God would take care of our two little babies now in heaven, we allowed the nurses to take her from us. Ryanne and I stepped over to Sophia's bed. We felt she knew what had just happened, so we tried to comfort her (and ourselves) with the thought of having two guardian angels now. Of course, we know that's not how things really work. We know Scripture teaches that angels are different creatures altogether from humans, and that when we die here, we don't become angels. But it was sweet to think of our little girls watching over us. We told Sophia how much we loved her and how proud of her we were. We told her not to worry about her sisters anymore because they were now perfect and at home with Jesus. We knew she probably wanted to be with them, but we were happy she chose to continue to fight here on earth with us.

Then we went back into the saddest room on the planet, the transition room. We sat in there and held each other. We cried in shock, disbelief, and utter sorrow. We had looked forward to having our triplet girls. They were such a blessing. We went from not having any kids to having three on the way. Ryanne had always said she wanted to have twins, and God had blessed her with triplets. Now, two were gone.

We were so sad thinking back on how much Reece and Vivian suffered the whole time they were here. We were equally disheartened that Sophia was still suffering. Since our desire to have children had led to this, we felt guilty for ever conceiving. We felt so helpless because we were never able to do a thing to ease their pain. We felt scared because Sophia still had a long way to go before she was well. We couldn't bear the thought of losing her too, but we realized it was a possibility.

Before Reece died, we had never given a thought to any of them not making it. We didn't know what to think anymore. At the same time, we realized we had hope because God had answered our prayers. It was just not the way we had envisioned. He took Vivian to heaven, and we knew she suffered no more. Heaven is better than earth, so that was the best-case scenario for her. She would no longer suffer in the NICU, and she would never suffer later in life. She was now complete and perfect and whole.

We Will See the Girls Again

Ryanne and I still had the joy of our eternal life, as well. Although we would miss our girls, we knew beyond a shadow of a doubt that because of our relationship with Jesus that we would see our babies again. One day we would be with them forever. God gave Jesus to die in our place on the cross to erase our debt of sin, rise from the dead, and reign eternally. We are no longer counted as sinners to be cast into everlasting hell, but now we may live with him forever. He healed our souls in eternity past, and we knew that he had healed our two babies eternally the moment they breathed their last breaths. That is the amazing grace that "transcends all understanding" (Phil 4:7).

Considering the grief we were experiencing because we missed little Vivian and Reece so much, I would hate to think what misery someone who has no faith must suffer during times like these. To wonder what happens when these bodies give out, to have no hope of living eternally in heaven, to have no assurance of seeing your loved ones again in a place where there will be no sickness, sadness, or crying ... what excruciating misery that would be. I am sure we could have made it through; people do every day. But I am so happy that we didn't have to face these difficult times without our blessed assurance in Christ.

Ryanne and I called our family and let them know the fate of our pretty Vivian. Those were not easy phone calls to make. Everyone knew that Vivian's condition had been severely compromised. I know they were apprehensive receiving a call from me in the first place, given the likely nature of a call. Everyone was devastated to hear my sad news.

In a matter of minutes, our parents and some of our church ministers were in the transition room with us. Valerie came also. When they arrived, we were holding sweet, little Vivian in our arms. It was awful holding our baby with no life left in her. She had been gone for nearly thirty minutes now. All we had left was her little body. Her spirit had moved on. Our parents wanted to hold her as well. They each took turns. Everyone tried to say comforting things, but nothing could be said that we hadn't already heard or didn't already know. "We can't fathom the mind of God." "His ways are higher than our ways." "They are better off now." Our pain was so intense. Intellectual knowledge of Scripture and belief in what it said didn't bring much respite to our suffering. Yes, we had faith and hope, but we hurt.

With everyone milling around and talking, the room quickly became crowded. The temperature in the room rose, as well. After several minutes, Ryanne and I noticed a turn from consoling talk to small talk—banter really, about today's schedules, ball games, and the like. We were not comfortable with this because our time of suffering was becoming a social meeting for many of the others. It stopped being a time of comforting each other in the wake of such a tragic loss. I called the nurse back to take Vivian. I wanted my daughter respected and I didn't feel that was happening. The nurse said she would lay Vivian back in her bed, and we could stop by and see her one more time if we liked. This was everyone's cue to disperse.

My parents left to return to work. Ryanne's parents, Valerie, Ryanne, and I decided to go home. We needed to get out of there for a little while. Ryanne and I stopped by Vivian's bed one last time, kissed her on the cheek, and told her goodbye. That was the last time we saw her. How awful to leave the NICU knowing that when we returned we would be visiting only one baby. But it was wonderful to be able to come back and visit one baby. We were very thankful to still have Sophia, even though we missed Reece and Vivian so much.

Sophia Needed Us to Be Strong

Ryanne had not eaten all day. I had eaten a small box of cereal, and that was it. For me, that's not a lot. We stopped by a local restaurant on the way home. It wasn't the best decision, considering our state of being. We were mentally and physically exhausted and anguished. I'm not sure why we thought we would be fit to go out in public one hour after our child had passed away. I guess we were trying to be machines, to keep chugging along, not missing a beat, for Sophia's sake. We hadn't taken any time to mourn for Reece, and now we were not taking time to mourn Vivian. We felt guilty for that, but we also felt that it was necessary. That may have not been the healthiest way to act, but it was the only way we could cope for the time being.

As soon as we sat down in the restaurant, an Elvis song came on through the speakers. Since Elvis music had been Vivian's "theme" music for the past two days, it was difficult for me to refrain from crying when I heard that song. The realization that I would not have the opportunity to sing to her again cut me deeply.

During the meal prayer, Ryanne and I got emotional. Any prayer time was difficult. We were thankful God had granted us salvation, each other, and our girls, but we were so confused about what was going on right now. It was hard to pray, but it was good to pray. During the meal, I ate everything in sight. Ryanne couldn't eat a thing. Our conversation was forced. We were so sad. We wanted our girls back, and we wanted Sophia to be healthy. After eating, Ryanne and I went home, took showers, and rested for a little while before returning to the hospital to see Sophia later that night.

It was difficult going back in the NICU and past the spot where Vivian had been. The night shift nurses were on duty, and they were cleaning up Vivian's bed to get it ready for another baby. A few nurses came by to offer their condolences, but for the most part, it was life as usual, like nothing had happened. I'm not sure what we expected. It's not like time could stop because we lost a second child. It was just hard to see most of the NICU staff act as if our baby had not died earlier in the day.

Our grief would have been all-consuming if we had not had Sophia to take care of. She did not need us to be weak and pitiful. We had to continue being there for her physically, spiritually, and emotionally. She needed Mommy and Daddy to be strong. For ourselves, we would not have been so strong. We quickly learned that as parents our lives must be secondary to the lives of our children. That was a blessing. To have a baby to pour ourselves into was a gift. Otherwise, we may have wallowed in our misery.

We didn't want to, but we went home from the hospital the night of Vivian's death. Now, our tiny Sophia was there all alone, with no sisters to keep her company.

Chapter 22

Power

A COMMON DEFINITION of *grace* is unmerited favor from God. We were at a place in our lives where we could have really used some of that. Ryanne and I certainly felt as if we had been loaded down with "unmerited punishment" instead. I guess our selfish-side seems to always look at God as if he owes us whatever we want, and when things don't go according to our plans, we get pitiful about it. A wonderful attribute of God, however, is that he will reveal his true nature, identity, and intentions if we truly seek him. We just have to be willing to open our hearts and minds to the possibility that there may be more to God than we currently understand.

Ryanne and I had come face-to-face with the reality that we didn't have all the answers and that we needed God's favor, understanding, knowledge, and wisdom to be made real to us. We needed him and his grace to see us through. We drew so much of our stamina during Vivian's last days and her death from 2 Corinthians 12:9: "But he said to me,

'My grace is sufficient for you, for my power is made perfect in weakness.' Therefore I will boast all the more gladly about my weaknesses, so that Christ's power may rest on me."

In this passage, Paul is explaining to the Corinthian church how God had given him "a thorn in my flesh, a messenger of Satan, to torment me." The thorn was to keep him humble so he would not become spiritually proud because of his lofty position in the church and because of his ability to see revelations and visions. Paul goes on to write in verses 9b-10: "But he said to me, 'My grace is sufficient for you, for my power is made perfect in weakness.' Therefore I will boast all the more gladly about my weaknesses, so that Christ's power may rest on me. That is why, for Christ's sake, I delight in weaknesses, in insults, in hardships, in persecutions, in difficulties. For when I am weak, then I am strong" (2 Cor. 12:9-10). God revealed to Paul that it was not up to him to be a superman. Rather, it was his responsibility and privilege to allow the Holy Spirit to be super through him and his weakness.

Blessed Are the Poor in Spirit

Ryanne and I were now totally weak. We needed God's strength badly during this time, and we sought his divine power to be made perfect in us. All of our lives we had been so strong in faith, determination, and personality. Now we felt as though we were completely deflated. We came to realize that it is at times such as these when God's Holy Spirit is allowed to work in us all the more fully.

During the Sermon on the Mount, Jesus says: "Blessed are the poor in spirit, for theirs is the kingdom of heaven" (Matt. 5:3). I've been in church for a good majority of my life, and I have heard numerous sermons on this passage of Scripture. However, I never understood what it really meant—not until we were given the opportunity to be made "poor in spirit." We had nothing of ourselves to depend on anymore. We couldn't have faith in circumstances. We had no power to change our situation through positive thinking. We had not been able to pray earthly healing on our girls. We were unable to change God's mind about letting us keep Reece and Vivian. We were at our lowest emotionally, physically, and spiritually. Like the little drummer boy in the famous Christmas song, we had no gift to bring. Yet, this is when God released the power, might, authority, strength and valor of the kingdom into our lives.

When we realized we didn't have anything to offer, God was able to work in our lives the most fully. When we were made less, he was made more. Even though we may not have felt like it at times, we knew the mighty Holy Spirit was at work in us because we were able to function in a sane manner even in the midst of the chaos in which we were involved. We stayed close as a couple. We didn't lose our faith in God. I was able to go to work. We didn't fight. We prayed. None of these were easy tasks at times, but through God's provision, we endured. We were "poor in spirit," and God blessed us with the riches of the kingdom.

This is the way he wants us all the time. Shouldn't we want the same for ourselves? Why do we ever want to feel as if we have all the answers, when we have the One who really does have all the answers willing to grant us his wisdom, knowledge, power, and strength? A dear brother in the faith and spiritual mentor of mine, Jerry Meeks, wrote us a letter to help explain these principles shortly after Vivian passed. Mr. Meeks and his wife had been foreign missionaries for years but were now home, working in local missions. They had lost a son a few years prior in an auto accident. They too knew what it meant to be poured out, not only from their experience of losing their son, but also from the years of serving in a foreign land. Mr. Meeks' letter is relayed below.

March 29

Dear Gabriel,

Last night I lay in bed thinking about you and your family. As I thought and prayed, I was reminded of the time I lost my most precious son and the deep pain and endless struggles that became a part of my daily life to this day. Often I wished someone would talk with me from a personal experience. If you will permit me, I would like to share with you some things I have learned from my personal grieving experience. My prayer is that somehow I might be able to help relieve you of some unnecessary pain and help shoulder you through this deep reality of soul torture. I'm sorry for your breaking heart, but at the same time I know that you are in a special situation where God can minister to you in a way unequaled in your past.

Because of the intangibility of your enemy, you feel helpless and depressively angry. Oh, if only this enemy who has struck an awesome blow to your daughters had a physical from, you would enter a fist to fist battle unequal in this age. But what an impossibility. Therefore, we children of Adam's race seek answers when we are in our deepest struggles. We think that if a battle cannot be realized to relieve our pain than certainly answers will. The truth is, you may ask a thousand questions but the answer will not come. After all, you may not agree with the answer and you would come to an impasse and the pain would remain as real as ever.

So what can you do to receive relief from your pain and grief? Please follow me closely. Jesus was a man of sorrows and very well acquainted with grief. He wants to be your Lord in your debilitating sorrow. God has a broken heart; he wants to walk at your side. The Creator understands his children's pain and he is prepared to re-create within you. Your pain is deeper than you can imagine and affects you on a level you have never known before. God's grace can reach that level. He wants to meet with you there. Your sorrow has taken you to a level where you have never experienced God's mighty grace and power. No one would ever choose this crisis in life. But from this point on your life has the possibility of living on a plain that you have never known. God chooses to walk with you personally in the deepest parts of our soul. You can trust him because he loves you with an unequaled, perfect love. Don't look for answers; God is the answer. If you will permit him to walk your trail with you, you will heal through the creative power of God and your heart will sing a new song. God will not push you and you don't need to push him. Let him love you as his suffering child. He will stay close to you as you lean on him. Can a suffering wanderer wish for more in this troubled world of flesh than that the Mighty Creator should walk at his side?

I want to restate more briefly all that I have said. He who has received deep hurt has received an unusual depth in his soul that can receive an unusual measure of the grace and power of God. Answers will not meet the need of your pain. The Great Creator and the Savior of grace and mercy, the One who was himself acquainted with sorrows, desires to walk with you today and tomorrow. His grace can match your depth of hurt. You can trust your precious daughters in the hands of our loving and almighty Father and Creator. You can trust his heart completely. My prayer for you (and your family) is that you will thrust yourself into the mighty arms of your heavenly Father and permit him to do a re-creation of life, love, power, and purpose. He waits for your complete trust and is prepared to bless and use you as a choice servant.

Your brother and fellow struggler,
Jerry Meeks.

Mr. Meeks's letter makes the point Jesus and Paul were making in their statements discussed earlier. We must be willing to allow God's love and power to live in and through us in order to live victoriously through suffering. No matter what situation we may face, Jesus has promised his provision in the form of his kingdom and power, if we only allow ourselves to be humbled before him and accept it. Knowing this, we have the opportunity to keep our faith, trust, and hope in God and his will, no matter where they take us, because we have the full confidence of the kingdom's power living through us.

Reflection Questions

1. Describe a time when God's power was truly at work in you.
2. How do you know that God was working in or through you?
3. What do you think the secret is to having the Holy Spirit live through you in a mighty way?
4. What steps can you take to make sure you rely more on God's power than on your own?

Chapter 23

Another Day ... Another Funeral

For it is God who works in you to will and to act in
order to fulfill his good purpose.
—Phil. 2:13

THE NEXT DAY we made Vivian's funeral arrangements.
My dad took us again. I was hesitant about Ryanne
going. I knew how upsetting the process would be for her,
but she insisted that she wanted to be there with me. The
funeral home owner came out and expressed his sorrow at
seeing me again. I assured him he wasn't nearly as sorry as
I was. We sat in a meeting room and started paperwork.

The funeral home was in a century-old house in downtown Spartanburg. The room we sat in was large and cool
in temperature. A portrait of the patriarch of this family's
business hung above the fireplace, eerily staring down over
the one-hundred-year-old room. Suddenly, a fire began
blazing in the fireplace, startling us all. We nervously laughed
it off and reasoned that the gas logs now roared because they
must have been on a timer.

The owner of the business took us through the unpleasantries of setting up Vivian's funeral service. We told him we hoped this was the last time we would see him for this purpose. He expressed the same sentiment and assured us he would pray for little Sophia.

We left the funeral home and returned to the NICU to see Sophia. She was now the single light shining in our darkness. Valerie and Dave picked us up from the NICU for lunch around noon, and we went to a new place downtown. We tried to carry on normal conversations and be cordial, but we didn't do a very good job. After lunch, we spent the remainder of the day with Sophia, trying not to think of what the next day would hold as it would be the day of Vivian's funeral.

Pastor DJ met with us and asked if we had anything in particular we wanted him to say or do at Vivian's service, or if we had any specific song or Scripture to be presented. Ryanne and I had been drawn to the passage from Job where, after having his family and all of his wealth taken from him, Job states: "Naked I came from my mother's womb, and naked I will depart. The Lord gave and the Lord has taken away; may the name of the Lord be praised" (Job 1:21). We thought it was amazing that Job had the faith in God to stay true to him although he had been smitten by God for no apparent reason. His story was inspiring to us, and we wanted to have that same strength and faith.

We had recently heard a song on the radio that echoes the words of Job. The words went like this: "You give and take away. But my heart will choose to say, Lord, Blessed be your name'" ("Blessed Be the Name," by Matthew Redman).

What a perfect song for little Vivian's service! Yes, we were terribly sad and disillusioned at what had happened in the lives and deaths of our daughters, and we were upset that Vivian and Reece had been taken from us. But as the song says, the Lord gives and the Lord takes away. It is important to remember that he had not just taken away; first he had given. We had three beautiful daughters, even if only for a short time, before two were taken. Their being given to us was an amazing blessing. Were we to praise God only during the good times of life and not during the bad? Was he not God in the midst of tragedy as he was in the midst of triumph? Was he not due our honor, admiration, thanks, and praise in the dark corners of his will as well as the fully lit courtyards?

It was difficult getting out of bed the morning of Vivian's funeral. We were facing our second funeral in three weeks. Ryanne said she didn't know how she was going to get through the service. She'd had the same thoughts earlier with Reece's funeral, but she had made it. She thought she could not face a second child's passing, but what alternative was there? She made it through those nightmares and held everything together for Sophie, herself, and for me. She was so strong. She still is.

I imagine the hole in her soul felt wider than the Grand Canyon and more expansive than the galaxy, but I praise God for filling that void in Ryanne's heart with his loving goodness and grace. She depended on God's strength and power, and he did not disappoint. His mercy and valor was imbedded in the character of my wife. As Jesus said to the rich man, "All things are possible with God" (Mark 10:27).

We felt much of the same emotions as we did when preparing for Reece's service. We had many of the same questions and thoughts, and we had to go through the same motions on deciding what to wear, selecting which mementos to leave at her grave, and so on. It was a distressful experience, just like before.

We had Vivian's funeral set up like Reece's. Everyone would be in place when we arrived at the last minute to take our seats. This time, Ryanne and I drove alone in her car as Valerie, Dave, and Savannah followed. However, when we arrived at the cemetery, all of our family was waiting for us by the car path. The other attendees were milling around—not exactly how we thought things would happen. Our family members greeted us as we exited the 4-Runner, and hugs and kisses abounded.

We made our way to the tent to be seated. It was surreal … again … to have all eyes on us as we approached the small, white casket with baby roses on top. The agony of the thought that the baby we held just two days ago was now in that box was all-consuming. It was all we could do to keep our composure. We didn't want to show any weakness to our family and friends—we wanted them to think we had it all together. We didn't want them to worry about us or give us a second thought. We wanted their attention to be given to the memory of little Vivian.

There Is Always a Blessing Somewhere

DJ did a great job with the service. His words added comfort and gave a sense of meaning to all the madness. It was our intent to have the attendees understand that—although we did not understand all of the things of God—we were not angry with him and we still blessed his name. We wanted our demeanors and the words of the service to echo our belief that it was of utter importance to follow the Lord during periods of loss as well as during times of abundance. Only by his Holy Spirit living in us and through us could we see the situation as such.

After the eulogy, DJ came from behind the podium to hug the family. It was like Reece's funeral all over again.

Ryanne and I got up and went to place some of Vivian's things by her casket. We brought her Pluto stuffed animal we bought at Disneyland when she was just a tiny little thing in Mommy's tummy. We also brought her children's Bible that we had been reading to her. It's not the easiest task in the world to leave keepsakes by your baby's casket. We told Vivian we would miss her and love her forever. Then we walked away. Everyone was quiet as they made a path for us to walk through the crowd. We looked down or straight ahead, not wanting to make eye contact with anyone. I helped Ryanne into her side of the car, and I got in the driver's side. On that cold, quiet March day, we drove away from the cemetery one more time.

Ryanne curled up in her seat and cried as we drove off. I was angry and confused. What about the crackheads who get pregnant and carry their babies full term? What about the teenage girls who deliver their babies in secret and throw them in trash cans? We wanted our girls, and we would have been great parents to them. Why was all this happening? Why couldn't things have turned out differently? I had no answers. I still do not. What I do have is comfort from the God who set all of this in motion. He knows what he is doing even if I do not. In him our hope is secure.

We didn't talk on the way to the hospital. We were drained. We missed sweet Reece and Vivian, and we were scared that Sophia could face the same fate. She was doing better, but so much had gone wrong recently. We didn't know what to expect. We didn't want to get our hopes up about anything again. We just wanted to take life one day at a time.

We were so ready to see Sophia when we arrived at the hospital. It was still tough entering the NICU with only one baby in there. We knew Reece and Vivian were no longer suffering and were in heaven now, but we missed them here on earth. The doctor that day came over to console us. The staff knew we had just gone to the funeral. The doctor told us not to worry about Sophia because she was doing well and she would be all right. It was nice to hear some good news.

Valerie, Dave, and Savannah were leaving the next day, so we went home early that evening to hang out with them. It was fun to see Savannah, but so difficult knowing we would never see Reece and Vivian grow to her age. It's not like we felt this way only with Savannah; we were sad when we saw *any* little girl. We wondered what our babies would have been like. What would we have dressed them in? Would we have made them wear the same outfits, or would we have dressed them differently? What would their personalities have been like?

We would not be going home with three little princesses; we would not have the chance to see two of our girls grow up. But we were glad God allowed us the ability to be pregnant and have the girls. Of course, the delivery and the events following were not ideal, but some people never get the chance to be pregnant, and others lose their children before birth. We got to see our babies and hold them. We feel blessed to have had that opportunity. No matter how bad life gets, there is always a blessing somewhere in the midst of the pain. The blessings can be like diamonds, difficult to find but worth looking for.

Chapter 24

Why Pray?

DURING THIS DIFFICULT time, Ryanne and I began to doubt the necessity of prayer. If God's will was set and we were totally at the mercy of his will, then why pray? In our culture, we are taught that we make our own destiny. "If it is to be, it's up to me" is a mantra that is ingrained in our psyches. But it is not accurate. If it were really up to me, then I would have changed the outcomes for my daughters. We understood all too well, based on our experiences with Reece and Vivian, that if Sophia lived another second, then it was all up to God, not us, not the doctors and nurses, not the medicines. He could make her live or die with or without any of our influence or actions.

We began feeling nervous about whether or not our prayers for Sophia were going to be answered. Considering that our previous prayers for a healthy and full-term pregnancy, for the health of Reece, and for the sparing of Vivian had been unanswered, we began questioning the necessity and validity of prayer. We wondered why, if everything in our lives is predetermined by God, should we bother to ask him anything? If he was going to make decisions regardless of our requests of him, why make requests? We definitely had a hard time reconciling what we had always believed to be true about faith, prayer, and God's plans, and the reality of our current situation. We were bewildered and grief-stricken because of everything that had happened that we truly didn't know what to believe anymore.

For nearly all of our lives, if we prayed for something, God graciously gave it to us. This included health, academic success, athletic ability, a good career, peace, patience, whatever. But now it seemed that our prayers were not getting through. Nothing we prayed for was being answered. Had we always prayed in vain, for no real reason, because all the things we prayed for were really just up to us to achieve through our own volition? That is what we began to believe. It seemed the only plausible explanation. Prayer obviously did not mean a thing, and there was no reason to engage in the practice. Thankfully, we became aware of a few truths that definitely helped us realize the error and danger of this kind of thinking.

God Yearns to Connect with Us

First and foremost, the wonderful revelation that God is constantly seeking out a relationship with us gave us great encouragement and insight into the world of prayer. The Bible is full of accounts of God attempting a meaningful and right relationship with humanity. He does not require us to find him; he searches for us. From Abraham to Jesus, it is proven that God wants to know us and for us to know him. He reached out to us before we ever reached out to him, and he still does so today. This proves that God wants to be intimately involved in our lives.

God wants to hear our requests and pleas. He yearns to connect with us. He wants us to pray. If this were not the case, then he would not bother communicating with us through his Sprit, Word, and natural revelation (Rom. 1:20). He would not have given us the ability to pray. The door would be closed, so to speak. Jesus would not have taught us how to pray as he does in the famous "Lord's Prayer" passage (Matt. 6:9-13). It is reason enough to pray because we can. Otherwise, it would be like ignoring a parent who has loved and provided for us since birth. It would be like shunning your favorite superstar who asked you out for lunch. The Creator of the universe, the lover of our souls, the bright, morning star, the Lion of the tribe of Judah, and the King of all creation has granted us the ability to communicate with him. We would be fools not to take advantage of that great, amazing, and humbling opportunity.

Even if God never granted one request in one hundred years of prayer, just to be able to ask anything of the heavenly Father is a treasure in and of itself. Prayer is not about getting what we can out of God; it is about drawing near to him and aligning our spirit with his. It is a blessing and tremendous opportunity to have the chance to pray. We should take advantage of it whenever we can do so.

All Things Work for the Good

We were also shown that God's will is always superior to ours. That is why God is still there, loving us and wanting our communication with him to continue—even when our prayers are not being answered in the manner we desire. Even when we prayed and our prayers were not answered, we had to trust it was in our and our girls' best interests why God chose to not answer our prayers according to the way we thought he should. It is important to realize that

God answered all of our prayers, but he always answered them in the manner he deemed necessary.

Sometimes, we are like children asking for cookies before dinner. God says no. He answers prayers, but it may not always be in the way we want him to answer. Even so, he wants us to have faith that he is good and that his will for our lives is what we really need, even if we don't see things the same way at the time (or ever). This truth is conveyed by Paul in Romans 8:28: "We know that in all things God works for the good of those who love him, who have been called according to his purpose." This promise allows us to wade through the mire of hardship and know that nothing will ever be able to "separate us from the love of Christ"—not "hardship or persecution or famine or nakedness or danger or sword" (Acts 8:35).

If we love God—if we are in a relationship with him— even when we are in the midst of the fires of sickness, death, divorce, job loss, bad relationships, addiction, or whatever the tragedy may be, we can know that somehow, someway, the challenges we face are meant for our good. They are ordained by the hand of the Almighty. We may not understand why, and we may not even want to learn the lessons being taught. Regardless, they will be for our best. This is a comfort and blessing for the believer.

God is for us all the time, and he will not act in a manner contrary to our interests. As James 1:2-4 reads, "Consider it pure joy, my brothers and sisters, whenever you face trials of many kinds, because you know that the testing of your faith produces perseverance. Let perseverance finish its work so that you may be mature and complete, not lacking anything." This passage teaches us that trials have a purpose. If all of our prayers asked God to deliver us from trials, and he always answered them to our expectations, we would never live through teachable moments and would never develop perseverance and a deeper faith. When he does not answer some of our prayers in the manner we wish for, he is actually being true to his Word. What a blessing that God stays true to himself and does not waver depending on our request du jour.

We Must Align with God's Will, Not the Other Way Around

Had Ryanne and I not grasped the above principles, we would have never seen the purpose of ever praying again. Perhaps we would have lost all faith. But the reality is that God is not like a TV. If we have a TV that turns on for ten years like clockwork and then suddenly it no longer turns on, we trash that TV and buy another one. It no longer works like we want it to, so we discard it and get one that does. God is not at our disposal. It is up to us to align with *his* will, not the other way around.

This always works to our favor in the long term. Grasping that concept gives us all the more reason to keep up the communication with God, even when the world (and often our selfish nature) tells us he's not listening, or doesn't even exist. The truth is we are his children and children often can't understand why their parents say no to some requests. But parents have valid reasons for their answer. God is no exception. We must trust him and his judgment.

The reality is that prayer is for us, to allow us to speak with the holy and mighty God, to allow him to speak to us, and to usher us into his glorious presence and the center of his perfect will. He does not need us to pray, but he desires it as any parent longs for communication with his or her child. May we be found to continue in prayer even when it is difficult to do so. God will never move or change, but we can move or change to be closer to him.

Reflection Questions

1. Have you ever entertained the thought that it might not be worth it to pray? What was your conclusion and why?
2. In your own words, why does God desire us to pray?
3. By praying, are we assured of having all of our prayers answered? Why or why not?
4. What constitutes an answered prayer?
5. Are all answered prayers to our benefit? How do you know for sure? What Scripture confirms your answer?

Chapter 25

Prophecy?

Woe to the foolish prophets who follow their own
spirit and have seen nothing!

—Ezek. 13:3

RYANNE'S BIRTHDAY IS April 16. This year it fell
on a Saturday. The night before, Ryanne and I stayed
at the Marriott in downtown Spartanburg. It was a fun
getaway from our normal routine. The hotel was closer to
the hospital than our home, and we liked that a lot. If we'd
had the money, we would have stayed at that hotel every
night because of its proximity to the hospital. Our room was
very nice, with a great view, lots of room, and a wonderfully
comfortable bed. We ordered room service and watched a
movie. It was a great twelve-hour vacation.

We awoke on Ryanne's birthday, ate breakfast, and took
the five-minute drive to the hospital to see Sophia. We
arrived there to see a birthday card addressed to "Mommy
from Sophia" on top of her incubator. The nurses had made
a little card and stamped Sophia's hand and foot prints on

it. It was the sweetest gesture! I was glad they thought of doing that—because I didn't. It truly made Ryanne's day.

The nurses let Ryanne hold Sophia as soon as we arrived. Getting to hold her was a big deal. It meant she was doing well enough to get out of her bed and into her mama's arms. Of course, she was still hooked up to everything, but at least Ryanne could hold her. The only other times Ryanne had been allowed to hold her babies was when Vivian was dying and after Reece was already gone. It was special to see my wife holding her little girl. I could tell that both ladies really liked that experience. We stayed at the hospital all day on Ryanne's birthday. Since we had eaten a late breakfast, we didn't go out for lunch. We just stayed by Sophia's side all day long.

Sophia was so cute, and each second with her made our day. She sometimes opened her eyes and stared at us. We loved that. Her eyes were so deep, dark, and blue. They were like the deepest water of the ocean. Seeing her eyes and Vivian's eyes was a great gift, for we never got the chance to see Reece's eyes. Vivian's eyes usually told a story of despair. She looked distressed all the time, and that was difficult to see. I wanted to erase her pain and suffering, but I was helpless. On the contrary, on most days Sophia's eyes looked calm, and she seemed to be progressing well.

When Sophia held our fingers, at times she would squeeze so hard. That was the best. It let us know that she was there and fighting hard. She was so beautiful and so strong.

Ryanne was extremely attentive to Sophia. It blew my mind seeing the attention to detail she had as a mother. I quickly learned there is a big difference between a mother and a father. Ryanne would see something she didn't like about the way Sophie was lying, or the way some wire was pressing on her, or a myriad of other problems that presented. She would ask me to call a nurse to fix the problem. As a dad, I didn't notice most of the stuff. If I did notice something, I would often think, *Oh, that's not so bad. It'll just make her tougher.*

Looking back, I must have been a moron to think that. She was only six weeks old, was born at twenty-four weeks, and weighed only 1.9 pounds at birth! She shouldn't have been alive, but she was. She was already tough enough. I am thankful to have a wonderful wife who cared so much about every little detail.

That night Ryanne's mom hosted a surprise party for her at my request. The party was nice, and Ryanne had fun. She deserved a night of recognition and pampering. She had been so strong and so steadfast; a party in her honor was past due. She was twenty-seven years old, the mother of three who had already buried two of the three, and hanging on to the last baby with all she had. What an amazing woman! But what a difficult way to start out her twenty-seventh year.

Kangaroo Holding

The next week was uneventful. I went to work each morning after visiting Sophia while Ryanne stayed at the hospital all day. Sophia was doing well and seemed to be growing stronger and stronger. We spent as much time as possible with our little girl.

Ryanne called me one day at work. I could tell she was very excited.

"I have good news!"

"Well, what is it?" I asked.

"You can hold Sophia anytime you want to now," she said. "They took her off the oscillator, so she doesn't have to be on a flat, hard surface anymore. You can hold her as long as you want when you get here!"

Before when we held her, it was only for limited amounts of time, and those times were few and far between. That was due to the fact that she had been on the oscillating ventilator. I liked the sound of "anytime you want" because I wanted to hold her so badly.

That evening, the nurses seemed excited that Sophie was off the oscillator and on a regular vent. This was a big step forward. It meant her lungs were maturing and getting stronger. Ryanne and I were excited for Sophia. It had been six weeks, and it was great to watch her taking baby steps ahead.

For some reason, I didn't get to hold Sophia that night. But I held her the next day. I remember holding her for a long, long time … like two hours. It was so great. I always felt a little guilty for holding her for so long because that meant Ryanne wasn't getting the chance, but my guilt didn't make me give her up any faster.

When Ryanne's turn came, the nurse suggested she hold Sophia skin to skin. They called it "kangaroo holding." The mother takes her shirt off and holds the baby against her bare skin. We were a little reluctant to try this. Sophia's oxygen saturation and heart rate would drop significantly when we moved her around. In addition, she had never been held vertically. She was always on her back or stomach. Those were the only positions that allowed the oscillating ventilator to work properly.

The nurses assured us Sophia would be fine. They said babies always did "very well" with the kangaroo hold; we had nothing to worry about. We trusted their judgment and agreed to try.

Ryanne took off her shirt, and we laid Sophia in Ryanne's arms so she could hold her against her chest. It was a sweet picture—for about a minute and a half. Then it turned scary. Sophia's stats suddenly declined. Her oxygen saturation and heart rate plummeted. She turned pale gray. This was not a good situation. Sophia was not getting the oxygen she needed. Her lungs were not developed enough to work properly in an upright position.

But the nurses told us not to worry. Sophia would soon stabilize. "Babies love this," they assured us. Some babies probably did, but Sophie was struggling.

We quickly realized that Sophia was not going to stabilize. Her stats plummeted even lower; her color went from gray to ashen, almost white. Ryanne and I were very frightened. The nurses were always calm and collected, but we could see they were getting nervous. They unhooked Sophia from the automatic ventilator and performed CPR, using a manual air pump while Ryanne held her. Next, they took Sophia from Ryanne's arms and laid her back in her bed so she could be flat and horizontal. This, along with the manual ventilation, allowed greater air pressure into her developing lungs.

We had seen this technique performed on Vivian and Reece when they were trying to revive them from cardiac arrest. The tension on the nurses' faces was palpable. The horror in our faces had to be even more obvious. We held our breaths, hoping Sophia would catch hers. After a few hour-long minutes, her heart rate, oxygenation and color returned to normal.

Ryanne and I were angry at ourselves for not following our parental instincts in that situation. We knew it wouldn't be good for Sophia to go to that upright position, and it *really* wasn't. She came close to dying that day. Needless to say, Ryanne and I were shaken. Our hearts were racing, our stomachs churned, and our souls were crying out in anguish. We were so scared of losing her, our last little baby. Ryanne and I desperately missed Vivian and Reece. We had resigned ourselves to the reality of bringing only

Sophia home. We didn't want to entertain the thought that she might not make it. That night we realized how fragile she still was, and that we really had no assurance she would survive, either.

Visions from Their Own Minds, Not from the Mouth of the Lord

The people around us, including family, friends, and hospital personnel, kept telling us not to worry about Sophia. They said things like, "God has answered my prayer, and I know Sophia is going to be fine." "She's gonna make it. God told me so." "I've prayed about this, and God has given me the answer that Sophia is going home with you. Don't even worry."

Instead of receiving peace from positive comments like that, Ryanne and I were hesitant to even listen to them. We didn't want to get our hopes up. Were these people false prophets? We knew God had not spoken to us or given us an answer as he apparently had to these others. In fact, we felt that if God had not chosen to assure us, then there was a good possibility he had not spoken to someone else. Maybe we were cynical, or maybe we were just being realistic. Sometimes I don't know the difference. In the book of the prophet Jeremiah, God passes his judgment on false prophets with these words:

> This is what the Lord Almighty says: "Do not listen to what the prophets are prophesying to you; they fill you with false hopes. They speak visions from their own minds, not from the mouth of the Lord. They keep saying to those who despise me, The Lord says: 'You will have peace.' And to all who follow the stubbornness of their

hearts they say, 'No harm will come to you.' But which of them has stood in the council of the Lord to see or to hear his word? Who has listened and heard his word?"

—Jer. 23:16-18

The context of these verses is not similar in any way to the situation we faced. Jeremiah was a true prophet of God, who was given God's message to speak against the evil being done in Israel in God's name. The people in our lives were only trying to deliver hope to us and not attempting to do evil. But these verses in the book of Jeremiah speak to the fact that it is not the best idea to speak prophecy in God's name unless he has designated you a prophet. Several people were assuming that role unwisely. Who were they to speak on behalf of God? Who were they to say who lives and who dies? We received no comfort from anyone's attempts to assure us that God told them Sophia would make it.

We did have hope in one promise. Whatever happened, we knew our baby would be taken care of—either here with us or in heaven with Jesus. We learned from the errors of the many that when a friend or loved one is going through the valley of the shadow of death, it is best to simply offer love, encouragement, and friendship rather than false hope. We are assured of only what God's Word has promised us: comfort when we need it and peace that surpasses all understanding. Assuring those things to the suffering is the best course of action. The reality is that we know those aspects of God's will are meant to be fulfilled. Other than that, we don't know what lies in the future. Had Ryanne and I not been grounded in the reality of Scripture, we may have taken everyone's "prophecy" as absolute truth. That would have been a dangerous place to be.

Some Pretty Strong Stuff

Soon after the kangaroo-holding incident, Sophia developed a nasty infection. The doctors weren't sure what bacteria were causing the infection, so they started her on what they called "some pretty strong stuff" to "cover all the bases." We didn't like the thought of giving her medicine without knowing exactly what needed to be treated, but the doctors said it was necessary to insure that the infection didn't get out of hand.

With any medication, kidney and liver functions can be affected. Unfortunately, Sophia's kidney and liver function were affected. Her urine output decreased once she started the medications, and her body began swelling ... and swelling ... and swelling. We were upset and concerned.

One day, one of the RTs tried to comfort us by saying that Sophia, although very swollen, was far from the worst case she had ever seen. One baby she'd treated had swelled so much that she couldn't see her eyes—she could see only slits in the swelling where her eyes were. All the nurse could see of that baby's nose was the little button tip. This gave us hope that Sophia was far from the worst case, even though she looked in pretty bad shape.

After six or seven days, Sophie's blood tests showed she was over the infection, so she was able to get off the heavy medication. The day the medication stopped, Sophie began eliminating again. Her swelling went down almost immediately, and she had more urine output in that one day than she'd had the previous week. She soaked through her diaper, her blankets, and her bed! Never have we been so happy to see so much pee. It was great seeing Sophie back to her normal size again. She seemed to feel better, too. I wonder if any of our "prophets" saw that coming.

Chapter 26

Discerning God's Will and Deciding If It Is Good

WHAT IS GOD'S plan? Is it always good and worthy of our submission? Sometimes, God's plan is thrust into our faces without our playing any decision-making role. An example of this is the passing of our daughters Reece and Vivian. There are other times when we are given choices to decide which path to take. Once on the path by force or choice, we must decide if we will accept the road and where it is leading.

One Sunday evening early in May, Ryanne and I were to go to my parent's home for dinner, but we had a hard time leaving Sophie. She'd had a tough time breathing that day. She had been on the regular ventilator for a week or so, but that particular day her oxygen saturation was not up to par, her heart rate had been a little lower than normal, and her blood gases (carbon dioxide content in her blood) were not as they should have been.

The RT assigned to Sophie that day decided she needed to go back on the oscillating ventilator. Changing her back would help her lungs inflate better. The doctor had noticed on her recent chest X-rays that Sophia's lungs were not inflating all the way. She was still too tiny and too weak to keep them fully inflated using only the regular ventilator.

It was nerve-racking to watch them change ventilators. They had to unhook Sophia from the regular ventilator for a couple of seconds before they hooked her up to the oscillator. A few seconds is not a long period of time, but when the only way you can breathe is not available to you, that few seconds becomes very precious. As Sophia held her breath, we held ours.

She made the switch with no major fanfare. Once back on the oscillator, however, her stats dropped even lower. That was not supposed to happen. The doctor, RT, and nurses could not understand why. They increased the air pressure of the ventilator, trying to remedy the situation. This meant that the air being forced into her lungs was moving in harder. The purpose was to inflate her lungs faster and more fully. After a few minutes with no change, they increased the pressures again.

Ryanne and I became nervous because before Vivian passed away, the doctor told us that he didn't want to set the pressures too high on her ventilator for fear that she might develop a pneumothorax—a hole in the lung. That was a worst-case scenario. There would be no air exchange on that lung's side, and that would overstress the other lung and her heart. It also causes the chest wall to fill up with air. Those events could cause a quick death.

The higher they increased Sophia's pressures, the higher our level of anxiety rose. It was obvious on his face and in his demeanor that the RT was getting anxious too. He was trying everything he knew to help her, but things were not going well.

After several minutes, Sophia finally stabilized, but her vent pressures were much higher than they had ever been.

Ryanne and I did not want to leave for dinner that evening during shift change because of the uncertainty of the situation. Ryanne especially had a great deal of uneasiness about leaving, but we went anyway. We could have stayed out in the lobby during shift change, but we chose to go on to my parent's house for dinner. Gabrielle and Luke, our niece and nephew, were there and wanted to see us. We wanted to see them too. I remember Ryanne crying as we drove to my parent's house. She was so worried about little Sophia.

"Something's not right," she said. A mother's intuition is rarely wrong.

Five minutes after we arrived at my parent's house, my cell phone rang, displaying the hospital's number. My heart dropped to my knees, and I felt my face flush. I nearly fainted. I was in the kitchen with my mom. Ryanne was in the den, playing with Gabrielle and Luke. I answered the phone. It was Georgie, Sophia's nurse from the day shift.

"Mr. O'Sullivan, this is Georgie," she said. "I wanted to call to tell you that a few minutes after you left, Sophia developed a pneumothorax. A hole developed in her right lung, which caused the air to leak into her chest cavity. Thankfully, we caught the problem quickly and were able to insert a needle into her chest and drain the excess air. The doctor was caught in traffic, but he's here now and is finishing a proper chest tube that will allow her body to heal. We've decreased her vent pressures and she's doing well."

"Should we come right away, even though it's not 8:00 PM yet?" I asked. Normally, we were not allowed back in the NICU until after shift change.

"Yes, definitely," Georgie replied.

I told mom and everyone else what had happened. Ryanne and I left promptly to go back to the hospital.

I knew a pneumothorax was a bad situation, but the nurse sounded so calm. Maybe I was wrong about the seriousness of a pneumothorax and we really didn't have anything to be concerned about. For that reason, we weren't panicked and we didn't speed to the hospital. However, we were upset for ever having left that evening. Ryanne knew deep down that we should have stayed, but I convinced her otherwise. I guess God thought it better we were not there when everything went down. At least, that is how I rationalize us leaving that evening. Since this scare, I have learned that when we are placed in the middle of situations where we don't necessarily know how to act, or when we are not one hundred percent sure what God's perfect will is, it is up to us to do the best we can with the wisdom God has given us by the bidding of his Spirit. After that, don't have any regrets.

All One Can Do Is Trust the Lord

As I have written previously, we don't know the will of God; only he does. We have to respond to life with the information we have been given and act with the knowledge we have. Proverbs 3:5-6 reads: "Trust in the Lord with all your heart and lean not on your own understanding; in all your ways submit to him, and he will make your paths straight." That is all we can do, and that is all God expects us to do. The writer of these verses in Proverbs expects us to be moving. That is why he uses the phrase "he will make your paths straight." When trying to decipher God's will in a situation, we need to keep moving. If we stop, we could develop paralysis by analysis and never proceed in any direction.

Ryanne and I had two choices: go to my parent's house for dinner or stay at the hospital. Sometimes life is like that—we simply pray and move. One of our choices could be a definite *yes*; the other a definite *no*. Often, God gives us choices that may be mutually good. In those cases, he expects us to use the faculties and wisdom he has given us to choose.

As soon as we walked through the doors of the waiting room—before we could even get to the phone to ring us in—the doctor came out the "in" door. He was wearing a surgical paper hat and a concerned look. We feared the worst. He explained that Sophia was doing well, she had stabilized, and they were almost finished with the clean up from her surgery. He would send someone out to get us as soon as Sophia was ready. He then went back inside the NICU.

Ryanne and I took a seat in the waiting room and held each other's clammy hands. A few moments later, our nurse from earlier that day, Georgie, came out with the nurse we had known prior to all this, Christina. They were holding hands and crying. Ryanne and I looked at each other, puzzled and frightened. Just a few seconds ago, the doctor said everything was fine, and now we had two nurses coming out clutching tissues? Ryanne began crying. We couldn't believe this was happening. How could things have taken such an awful turn in mere minutes? The doctor said Sophia was fine only two minutes before!

"What's going on?" I asked.

Through tears the nurses assured us that Sophia was fine. They were crying because they had been so scared about almost losing her. It was a relief to learn we had jumped to the wrong conclusion but disturbing to see how shaken the nurses were over Sophia's condition. They went on to explain the course of events.

One of the respiratory therapists was checking Sophia shortly after we left and recognized that something was wrong. The RT made a judgment call and ordered everyone to immediate action. Christina and Georgie shared that they had never seen their team work so fearlessly and efficiently. Since this occurred right at shift change, the new nurses were performing the procedures, and a vast majority of the nurses who could have opted to go home joined hands, circled up by Sophia's bed, and prayed for her.

What a blessing to have nurses who boldly prayed for our little girl! Not only did they pray, but they prayed beside her bed when they had every right to be on their way home to their families. We were so grateful for such a devoted and professional staff taking care of our baby girl!

Discerning God's Plan

When thinking about these events, I have seen more parallels regarding following and discerning God's perfect will. In order to decipher the correct path to take, we must be in tune to our surroundings and our options. Had the RT been oblivious to Sophia and merely focused on getting her stuff ready to go home, Sophia would surely have died that day. Every day in life we are placed in circumstances requiring our direct and immediate action. We are called to recognize the right path that God has laid out for us, act accordingly, and avoid the wrong path altogether. Had the RT not been in tune with "right" and "wrong" behaviors of breathing, stats, and visual cues, things would have turned out differently for Sophia. The fact that the RT was aware made all the difference in the world.

Consider this: What has God placed in your life right now, directly in front of you, that he wants you to do to complete a portion of his plan for your life? What are some concrete ways to discern the Lord's plan? The apostle Paul writes, "Therefore, I urge you, brothers and sisters, in view of God's mercy, to offer your bodies as a living sacrifice, holy and pleasing to God—this is your true and proper worship. Do not conform to the pattern of this world, but be transformed by the renewing of your mind. Then you will be able to test and approve what God's will is—his good, pleasing and perfect will" (Rom. 12:1-2).

These two powerful verses tell us that if we are living as sacrifices to God, if we are making a concerted effort to live differently than the world, and if we are allowing his Holy Spirit to renew our minds, then—and only then—will we able to actually know the will of God. The words *test* and *approve* are crucial. Paths laid out before us need to be evaluated and confirmed through spiritual lenses. Why? Because even though God's will is God's will and he certainly knows which path we will ultimately choose, there is obviously a path that is the best for us.

The Bible teaches us that "your Father in heaven is not willing that any ... should perish" (Matt. 18:14). If all of humanity made him their Lord, no one *would* perish. But the reality of his ultimate will is that since he has given men and women free will, some choose him and some do not. Both options are there for everyone. Therefore, it is imperative that we stay in tune with the Holy Spirit so we may make the appropriate decisions that are in line with God's "good, pleasing and perfect will."

Back to the NICU

A few minutes later, we were called back into the NICU. Sophia looked good, despite having a tiny tube inserted into her right chest wall. The tube was hooked up to a water-pressurized vacuum to keep the air out of her chest wall and allow her lungs to inflate and deflate properly while the lung tissue repaired itself. The doctor told us he would take out the chest tube within twenty-four to forty-eight hours. It would take that long for her lung tissue to heal.

The main concern now was Sophia's brain, It could have been adversely affected from a lack of oxygen between discovery and correcting her lung problem. Sophia's brain didn't need any more damage. The doctor also warned us that the chest tube insertion site could possibly develop an infection, as with any puncture of the skin. But he was hopeful that all would be fine. Sophie would have another brain ultrasound in the next day or two. In the meantime, they planned to keep her sedated and lying on her back so she could heal and rest.

Once all the explanations were complete, we were able to spend time with Sophia by ourselves. She was such a tough little girl and fought so hard. She had so much against her, but she didn't give up. How easy it could have been for her to say, "Forget this. I am miserable here, and my sisters are now made perfect and whole in heaven. I'm going to be with them!"

She could have given up, but she hung on, not knowing what kind of pain and discomfort she would face the next day. We were so proud of her, and we let her know it. We cried as we told her how sorry we were that we had left her earlier when she was not doing well. We felt like bad parents for leaving her side when she was struggling.

A few minutes later, the doctor came over and asked if we wouldn't mind sitting down with him and the RT who had made the vent change that ultimately caused Sophie's pneumothorax and almost killed her. Apparently, the RT was devastated that the call he made led to almost losing our third child. That was understandable.

We went into the transition room and sat down. The RT was crying. The doctor asked us to console this young man and talk him out of quitting. We didn't speak for a moment.

We were searching for an answer from the Lord as to how to handle this situation. My first inclination was to pat him on the knee and tell him to toughen up. I wanted to get back to Sophia. Ryanne felt the same. After all, we were still dealing with the grief of already losing two infants and the near loss of our third only moments before. Yet, in our moment of silence and quick, quiet prayer, God impressed upon our hearts that it was his desire that we offer a glimpse of the hope that we had to this young man. After all, we did not blame him for the events that had just taken place.

We felt similar to Job, who ends up being the voice of godly reason to his entourage after losing his family, fortune, and health, though they should have been the voice of godly reason for him. Certainly, Job should have received comforting counsel from his friends, but God ordained that Job would be the one expressing truth more so than those around him. Likewise, God appointed that time for Ryanne and me to share the love and peace of Christ with a virtual stranger. We were angry that we were asked to leave the bedside of our daughter in order to grief counsel this adult man, but thankful that God chose to use us in that situation despite our attitudes. As believers, being in the center of God's will often means that our personal wants will be usurped by God's plan. Just ask Jesus. He didn't *want* to be beaten and killed on a cross. Yet, submission to the schedule of the Almighty will always be rewarding in the long run.

Some Major Setbacks

We rose early on Monday and went to check on Sophia. She was doing well. Her chest X-ray that morning showed that healing needed to continue, so they would maintain the chest tube insertion awhile longer. They started her on some

strong antibiotics again. The doctor was taking precaution-
ary measures just in case she developed an infection from
the chest tube site. Sophia didn't have an infection that they
could tell, but he was giving her medication in case she had
one that was not yet detectable. Sophia's brain ultrasound
from that morning did not show any changes, and that was
great news. We still believed God would completely heal
our little Sophia Renee. She was going to come home. We
just knew it.

The twenty-four to forty-eight hours to heal her lung
turned into six days. It took that long for her lung to heal.
After they removed the tube, they put a few little stitches
in to close up the hole. Her lungs were now healed, and her
brain was showing minor improvements. It appeared as if
the clots were resolving in her brain, which was a miracle.
Grade III bleeds rarely see improvement. We were so excited
at her progress! Sophia had a couple of good and promising
days after her lungs healed. Things were really looking up
after these few major setbacks.

Unfortunately, after those few good days, her urine
output waned again. She went an entire day without
urinating. It was just like the last time she was put on strong
antibiotics.

The next day, the doctor decided to try some medicinal
measures to make her go to the bathroom. Sophia was put
on a diuretic, but nothing happened. Her fluid levels were
changed and she was given more diuretic, but it didn't help;
she began swelling again. The doctors told us she must have
an infection. The body's urine output often significantly
decreases as a result of an infection. They increased her
antibiotics again.

Next, Sophia's fluid levels and concentrations were
changed and they gave her more and different kinds of
diuretic. Nothing worked. She continued swelling … and

swelling ... and swelling. All Ryanne and I could do was pray and pray and pray. One week passed. No urination. Sophia was getting larger and larger from the fluid accumulating in her body. The nurses and RTs tried to comfort us with the same speeches about her not being the worst they had seen. All the while, Sophia's swelling increased. Nothing was working, not even our prayers.

Every waking moment we weren't talking to Sophia, each other, or someone on the NICU team, Ryanne and I were pleading with God. We begged him to heal our daughter. We asked him to continue being our strength. We were weak, and we needed him to be strong for us. We knew he was the Healer, and we desperately needed him to act in Sophia's favor. Yet, the more we prayed for her healing, the worse she got. We didn't understand. We thought that when a child of God asks for something that certainly must be within his will, then God was supposed to answer in their favor. This was not shaping up to be the case, and it hurt us to the core.

The Almighty Is Beyond Our Reach and Exalted in Power

I realize now that just because we want something and believe our desire must be in God's will does not mean it is. In the Garden of Gethsemane, just before the Lord's crucifixion, Jesus said, "Father, if you are willing, take this cup from me; yet not my will, but yours be done" (Luke 22:42). He prayed that God would "take this cup from me," but God did not do it. Surely, the disciples and Jesus' mother and friends prayed fervently for him the night he was arrested that God would deliver him from the hands of evil men. But God didn't.

Would Paul not have prayed for safety on his missionary journeys? Yet, he was often beaten, shipwrecked, and without food, shelter, and water. Do the Scriptures not teach that Job prayed daily for his children, yet they were all struck dead without warning? The point is that we are not God. Job 37:23 states that "the Almighty is beyond our reach and exalted in power." That says it all.

Mother's Day arrived, and it was quite the emotional day. My sweet wife was the mother of three beautiful baby girls, but now only one remained. I hoped the day would be extra special for her, but I knew it would be a tough one. I bought Ryanne a necklace charm in the shape of a baby shoe. It was white gold and porcelain (painted pink) with a diamond for the bow. I also purchased her a pink T-shirt with white letters that read "I Love Mom" from Sophia. I gave them to her before we went to the hospital that morning. Ryanne loved the necklace charm and she wore the shirt and necklace to church that morning, along with a nice jean skirt and sandals. She looked so pretty. She was such a *Hot Mama*!

At the hospital, the nurses had made Ryanne a Mother's Day card from Sophia with her hands and feet stamped on it. It was a cute card and much appreciated. Those ladies were so thoughtful. It made our day even more meaningful.

Ryanne and I left awhile later to eat lunch with our parents. We hurried through lunch and rushed back to see our baby. We wanted to spend as much time as possible as a family, the three of us, on this special day. Although she was still swollen, the nurses allowed Ryanne to hold Sophia. She had not used the bathroom in over two weeks. Nevertheless, Sophia seemed to be doing pretty well. Ryanne enjoyed being able to hold her little girl on her first Mother's Day, although this was not the way we expected it to be. She was still supposed to be pregnant, and next year she would have celebrated her first real Mother's Day with three healthy babies who would have been nearly a year old at the time.

We were quickly coming to the realization that our perceived wants, needs, hopes, desires, and aspirations did not necessarily match God's wants, needs, hopes, desires, and aspirations for us. This was a harsh reality to face, but it was reality nonetheless. We had to learn that God's plans are always good, even when we can't see the "good" for the "bad."

God Is a Refiner

A song playing on the radio during this time was one by Natalie Grant entitled "Held." The lyrics speak of how it feels when "your sacred is taken way." At first, the verse seems to be referring to a precious baby, a mother's sacred child being taken from her too soon. We could relate. Yet, when contemplating the full set of lyrics, we realized that "your sacred" means so much more. For us, God was our wish-granter, and we had the notion that our sacred desires were naturally his sacred desires. As our two girls were taken, these sacred things were taken away from us. Sophia was struggling, and this sacred thing was in jeopardy. God was stripping us of what we held dear, but that was a good thing because what we held sacred was a lot of incorrect thinking, knowledge, and theology.

God is a refiner, always striving to make his precious children more pure and holy. At times, this process can be painful and confusing. When he places us in the fire we can be fully confident that God's love for us is not lacking just because we are going through a struggle. We are certain that his love knows no bounds, and that his will is good and ultimate. How can we be so certain of this when life's cards are stacked against us? Consider this: He gave himself up for us and died in our place while we were his enemies.

"But God demonstrates his own love for us in this: While we were still sinners, Christ died for us" (Rom. 5:8).

Christ's death means that even though we are completely unworthy, we can approach his throne of grace. The shed blood of Christ makes us worthy. He took the wrath we deserved so we could spend eternity with him ... and with our girls. This is why Job could say, "Though he slay me, yet will I hope in him" (Job 13:15). Obviously, Job did not want God to slay him. Rather, he was saying that no matter what happened to him, his confident expectation was in the purpose and person of God. Job had the confident expectation that though life was terrible for him, God's will was still good and perfect and actually in his best interest.

Job's amazing ability to continue on with a steadfast heart developed his character when he was in the midst of such disheartening circumstances. He did not say his hope was in life or circumstances; it was in the Lord of this life, the Lord of his circumstance. The psalmist asks, "Why, my soul, are you downcast? Why so disturbed within me?" Then he says, "Put your hope in God, for I will yet praise him, my Savior and my God" (Ps. 42:5). The psalmist has the same idea as Job. Since God is our Savior, we can put our hope *in him*.

Our hope does not have to be, nor should it be, placed in anything or anyone else. The apostle Paul wrote, "For everything that was written in the past was written to teach us, so that through the endurance taught in the Scriptures and the encouragement they provide we might have hope" (Rom. 15:4). In this passage, we find our hope can be placed in the truth of the Word of God. Our life events may not be what we expect them to be—and they may change from bad to worse at times—but we can be encouraged knowing that God's Word and God's plan do not change. They are good as they stand, and they give everlasting life to all who believe.

I have called this chapter "Discerning God's Will and Deciding If It Is Good." The title is perhaps somewhat misleading in the sense that discerning God's will and deciding if it is good might seem like a linear process. The truth is that they are often intertwined in real life. As we figure out what God's plans are, though, we are fortunate enough to know for certain that they are good and perfect. We just have to accept and trust in that truth.

Reflection Questions

1. How can you argue that God's will is good when it allows for death, destruction, pain, and suffering?
2. What Scriptures give you the confidence that God really loves you and has your best interests at heart?
3. What are some examples from the Bible that teach us that God's will is sovereign and good, despite a worldly view that would say otherwise?
4. Is God good? What evidence do you have to prove he is?
5. Write a prayer praising God for his good, pleasing, and perfect will, and ask him to help you stay in the center of it.
6. What are some real ways to help you discern God's plan?

Chapter 27

The End

The grace of the Lord Jesus be with God's
people. Amen.

—Rev. 22:21

AFTER MOTHER'S DAY, Sophia's condition began to
worsen. She was not eliminating her waste at all. Every
morning, we came in and asked if she had urinated. In the
middle of the night we would awaken, call the NICU, and
ask the same question. Sophia continued swelling. Her
doctors consulted each other and also consulted pediatric
kidney doctors. They read books and scoured the Internet.
They increased her fluids. They decreased her fluids. They
changed this. They changed that. Nothing.

After a few weeks, about mid-May, Sophia had become
the baby the nurses said wouldn't happen. She was the
worst-case scenario. She was so swollen you couldn't see
her eyes, only little slits in the swelling where her eyes were.
Her nose was just a cute little button. Her nostrils were
completely closed off due to the swelling of her top lip.

Her arms were permanently situated in the "touchdown" position. Sophia was so swollen that neither she nor I could move her arms down by her side. She should have weighed three or four pounds, but her weight had increased to over eight pounds. Her condition became so bad that she began seeping fluid through her skin. The nurses had to change her bed linens several times each day to keep her dry and comfortable. Her IVs pushed out because of the swelling, and it became more and more difficult for the nurses to get them back in. They called a pediatric surgeon in from a nearby town to put a direct line into the vein going to her heart so they wouldn't have to keep trying to stick her with the IVs.

It was a surgical procedure, and seeing Sophia prepped for it was a little frightening. Several OR nurses came into the NICU with a roller cart full of equipment. They were dressed in sterile scrubs. I thought the surgeon would come in and do his thing by himself. I didn't realize he would have such an entourage. All of the build-up made us realize this procedure was a bigger deal than we expected. While they operated on our Sophia, Ryanne and I waited in the transition room, kneeling and praying.

Much to our pleasure, the pediatric surgeon was quick at his work. We expected him to take a long time after we saw all of his accompanying crowd and his vast array of equipment. We expected a lengthy ordeal because he told us there was a possibility he couldn't even get the line in because she was so swollen. We were grateful that neither of these was the case. He finished in about twenty minutes, and we were able to be back by her bedside.

Sophie didn't seem to mind the surgery at all. It apparently didn't bother her that she had a line inserted into her chest that went straight to her heart. All of her levels, blood pressure, oxygen concentration, and heart rate were normal. I was so proud of her. She was such a fighter!

A day or two after the surgery, Sophia had to have a new IV put in. Usually, the nurses made us leave when they inserted a new IV. They didn't want us having to watch them sticking our baby several times with a needle until they achieved a successful line. That day, we were not asked to leave. No doubt the nurses realized we had witnessed enough disturbing things already, and this IV procedure would be no big deal to us.

Sophia was no longer in an incubator but in a regular bed out in the open. The nurses told us they left her out in the open in case they had to get to her quickly. That was a very sobering thought. As the nurse was trying to get the IV in Sophie's leg, I was able to stand beside my daughter and hold her tiny hand. When the nurse stuck her leg, Sophie squeezed my finger so hard. Her heart rate never dropped, and her oxygen levels remained normal. That told us she was not really distressed by the procedure. She just squeezed Daddy's hand and took the pain. After several attempts, the nurses finally found a vein and inserted the IV. Sophia and I were both glad about that. Ryanne was excited too. I knew she was worried I would pass out watching them stick my daughter. It certainly wasn't pleasant to watch, but I was grateful to have been there next to my little baby to hold her hand.

Alternative Techniques

The following week did not bring any positive change for Sophia. Still, Ryanne and I never gave up hope. Every day, we came to the hospital expecting Sophie to have gone to the bathroom the night before. Every day we were disappointed, but we never gave up hope. We believed in Sophia's resilient spirit and in God's power to heal.

It became obvious to us that traditional medical techniques were not going to work favorably for our daughter's condition. We decided to take matters into our own hands as much as we could. Being involved in the natural healing arts, I couldn't bear the thought of standing by any longer and watching. I had to take a more active role in my baby's health care. One of the massage therapists at our office told us about a friend of hers who worked in the hospital. She said the lady did a certain massage technique that was supposed to help with fluid elimination. We talked with the doctors, and they were okay with her working on Sophia. They admitted they were at the end of their ropes. It wouldn't hurt to try anything at this point.

The massage therapist, Ann, was gracious to give of her time to work with Sophie. When Ann worked on her, we could tell that Sophia liked the massage. Her heart rate and oxygen saturation levels both increased. The NICU staff were a bit wary of an "outsider" coming in and doing anything to "their baby," but we thought the massage was worth a try, so we dealt with the attitudes and the questioning stares the best we could. We were a little hurt that some of the staff seemed to judge us when all we were trying to do was help our little girl. Their methods were not working. Why were they not open to trying something else?

I brought in a cold laser to do some acupuncture points on Sophia for waste excretion. She did fine with this too. I adjusted her and worked on her little spine, particularly in the area that supplied the nerves to her kidneys.

Sophia had been lying on her back now for over two weeks. Each morning, I did exercises with her, moving her little arms and legs as much as I could. I know she had to be sore and stiff. I hoped the adjustments and exercise helped with that. Then we would pray together. We prayed for her and for the other babies in NICU. Then I would read little Bible stories to her. We had such special times together in the early morning, just Sophia and I.

Unfortunately, none of the alternative techniques we tried worked. Sophia had no urine output. Her outlook was getting grimmer by the minute. It was a Tuesday when Ryanne called me at work and said the doctor wanted to talk to us, but it was nothing urgent. I immediately left the office anyway.

When I arrived at the NICU, I found Ryanne upset. The chaplain had stopped by to chat, and it was like a game of "Twenty Questions." The chaplain had asked Ryanne if we were getting the nursery ready, whether we had bought a lot of clothes, and so on. She was asking some weird questions, considering it was looking like Sophie wasn't going to make it out of the NICU alive. Ryanne said it was like the lady was quizzing her to see if she realized the gravity of the situation.

That was not a good day for Ryanne to be barraged by such questions. The night before we had received an email from the company where we had ordered Sophie's crib bedding. The email said the company was out of the pattern we picked. That was difficult news to take because we had been looking for the perfect print since January. Now, the one we finally decided on (after two of our babies had already passed) was not available. Was this an omen? Or was our faith being tested? Or was none of it related? We didn't know, but it surely didn't seem good.

We Were Being Too Positive!

Soon after I arrived, the doctor asked us to join him, a nurse, the chaplain, and an RT in the transition room. He told us there was now a zero percent chance that Sophie would live. The end could come in minutes, or it could be a few days. He wanted to be sure we understood the severity of her condition, because he felt that maybe we didn't. Ryanne cried. I fumed. She cried because she was fuming.

It was an awful thing to hear the prognosis put to us this way. We knew Sophia's chance of survival was low, but to hear someone say it so brusquely was not easy. I was angry. It was obvious the chaplain was not there to comfort Ryanne. She was there to obtain information from her, just as Ryanne had thought. I was also mad because they were treating us like we had just jumped off the turnip truck and into the NICU.

What that meeting boiled down to was that we spent thirty minutes away from our baby in the transition room for *another* conference. This time because people felt we were being *too positive*. We explained that we were completely aware of Sophia's poor outlook. However, that didn't mean we would go into our baby's presence every day and act as if it was the day she was going to die. As long as she was with us, we were going to keep hope alive for her. We would continue having faith that God could and would (if he wanted to) perform a miracle for Sophia. We would not act in any other manner. After a half hour of convincing the group we knew Sophia was facing her last days, we left the transition room and went back to see our baby.

Although I was angry, I was glad the doctor had leveled with us. If Sophia really had only minutes to survive, then I wanted to spend as much time as I could with her. Ryanne felt the same way. I called my office and informed them that I would be taking the rest of the week off.

Was This Further Punishment?

All we could do now was pray. Everything that could be done medically to save Sophia had been done. Her healing was in God's hands, and in his hands alone. Ryanne and I wholeheartedly believed that God could heal her, and why shouldn't he? We had been faithful to him. We aren't perfect, but who is? If this was punishment for not asking forgiveness in some area of our lives, why would God punish us with the death of Sophia? How could a loving God allow us to suffer any more than he already had? Wasn't taking two of our girls enough? We reasoned that it had to be enough. But who were we to decide what Almighty God should or shouldn't do with our or our children's lives?

During this introspective time, Ryanne and I reflected back to Abraham and Isaac. We felt we were in a similar situation with Sophie. We had to choose if we would deny God and his sovereignty when life didn't make sense, or submit to his will even if it cost us that which we held most precious. Ryanne and I held our babies most precious, and God had chosen to take two of them. Would we remain faithful, as Abraham had? Would we submit to God, or would we shun him?

Ryanne and I felt that we had accepted the blows of God to our lives without complaining. Surely, he would allow us take Sophia home, and she would be totally healthy and normal. We had learned our lesson about his sovereignty and our place in relation to his majesty. We knew he was almighty, and we were but clay in his hands. We believed that God would choose to heal little Sophia because he had seen the change in us. We were no longer the same two people who used to be confident in ourselves and our joyous lot in life as much as we were confident in him. We were now broken jars, poured out like water. God had to recognize this in us and heal her for us, we thought. Deep down, however, we were frightened that Sophia was nearing the end and that all our prayers and spiritual reasoning and bargaining meant nothing. Each day her heart rate dropped a few points. Her oxygen concentration and blood pressure slowly diminished.

The next week we stayed at the hospital constantly. The transition room was reserved for us because Sophia was doing so poorly. Sometimes we would leave to eat, or go home to take a shower and change clothes. Other than that, we were planted in the chairs beside Sophia's bed. Ryanne was amazingly strong and took such good care of Sophia by doing many things for her that only the nurses used to do.

Our Parents See Sophia

That week, we decided it was time to let our parents see little Sophia again. They had seen her twice, but it was only a brief visit on the days Reece and Vivian passed. We knew it had to be awful for them not to have had the opportunity to spend time with their grandchildren, but we did what we felt was in the best interest of the girls.

We called each set of parents and arranged a night when they could come and see their grandbaby. We cleared it through the NICU. Considering Sophia's condition, they were totally cooperative. We laid down three ground rules for the parents before they came in. First, there was to be no crying. We didn't want Sophia feeling any negativity. Plus, we didn't want to start crying ourselves. Second, there was to be no giving up hope based on what they saw. God could turn her around. Third, they could not tell anyone how pitiful Sophia looked. She was swollen and had stitches, bruises, and holes in her skin. She looked miserable. It was heartbreaking. Our parents agreed to the rules, and we let them come in two at a time.

They were happy for the chance to spend some time with Sophia. We explained what the monitors and wires and tubes meant. I'm sure it was overwhelmingly sad for them. It certainly had been for us those first few days. Our parents tried to be strong and positive, but we could tell they were having a difficult time. They hurt badly for Sophia and for us. We knew they wanted to stay by her side all night as we did, but everyone did a great job of sharing their time. We were proud to have such wonderful and unselfish parents.

No Chest Compressions

Saturday was an especially difficult day for Sophia. We almost lost her a couple of times, but she kept bouncing back. When Vivian's heart rate had dropped below eighty, they started chest compressions. The doctors said Vivian's heart rate was too low for her to get the oxygen she needed, and she was brain dead at anything below eighty beats per minute.

However, with Sophia, the doctor said it would be unwise to do chest compressions for a couple of reasons: Compressions would not sustain her life but only prolong her death. The condition of her swollen body and stretched skin would cause tears to her skin. Ryanne and I did not want her to suffer any more than she already had, so we told him not to perform chest compressions if it came down to that.

Sophia was not responding to anything now. A day or two before she would squeeze our hands every now and then; now she did nothing. She just lay there, virtually lifeless.

The nurses asked us if we wanted to give her a bath. We did. They had been putting powder all over her to help combat the moisture that was seeping from her skin and settling in her little fat crevices. The powder was antibacterial to help eliminate sores. Because of the powder, she was covered in yellow gunk from head to toe. She also had dried blood and afterbirth still caked on in some places. She had never even had a sponge bath. Her skin had been too fragile until now.

The nurses brought us a pail of warm, soapy water, a couple of sponges, a T-shirt, and Q-tips. Those were our bath-time tools. We had to be very gentle, but we were able to get her pretty and clean. She definitely liked taking a bath. We could tell she was happy to be fresh and clean. It was long overdue. Three months is a long time to go without a bath, especially for a prissy little girl. Unfortunately, right after her bath, we had to put the powder back on, so she got gunky again. At least she was clean and sparkly for a few minutes.

Sophie's heart rate continued to drop. She was going through a lot of the same things Vivian had gone through during her last days. Vivian had slowly faded away into eternity. It looked like Sophia was doing the same, but we kept praying that God would turn things around.

Ryanne and I took turns holding her. Sometimes, I would read to her from her little Bible. Sometimes, I would read to her from my Bible. We prayed with her and for her. We sang her song, "My Sophie Amor." Ryanne held Sophie, and I would kneel beside them and hold Ryanne.

We cried.

Why Wouldn't God Hear Us?

We didn't feel that we had the strength to go through another death of one of our children. We wondered why God wouldn't hear and answer our prayers for our baby girl. We couldn't understand why our communication with him had apparently been broken. Why had he chosen us to smite? What had we done wrong? After thinking about it, we realized that it was not necessarily anything we had done. As God's creation, he can do whatever he chooses with us. He does as he pleases to fulfill his purposes and bring himself glory. God's plans will prevail. As children of the King, we are subject to his wishes, even if they may be far from pleasant for us. Again, think of Jesus' situation.

In the fourteenth chapter of Mark's gospel, we find the account of Jesus' prayers in the Garden of Gethsemane the night before his crucifixion. He prayed three separate times that God would let the suffering he was about to endure pass from him. In essence he was asking, "God, why? Why must I go through this? Why can't we figure out another way to save the human race from themselves? Why can't we devise another plan to bring you ultimate glory and to show your grace, mercy, love, and forgiveness? Why can't we do anything except for the thing that I am about to do?"

Jesus was asking, "Why?" His human nature did not agree with his heavenly plan. He knew he did not deserve to go through the torture he would soon endure. He wanted another answer than the one set before him. He wanted another destiny than the one he was facing. He knew his Father was sovereign over all and that anything was possible with him—so why this?

At the end of a long and sleepless night, when his soul was in such utter turmoil that he sweated drops of blood, a night much more difficult (but similar) to ones Ryanne and

I had recently faced, Jesus said, "Father, if you are willing, take this cup from me; yet not my will, but yours be done" (Luke 22:42). Jesus accepted the cup given to him to drink. That cup was filled with an unjust arrest, ferocious beatings, and a tortuous death on the cross. The Lord Jesus never did anything to deserve what he endured. He did everything God ever asked of him and nothing outside of that. He was perfect. Yet, his lot in life included abject misery. Considering the injustice of Jesus' execution, the "unfair" sufferings we go through on earth do not seem as awful.

The amazing thing is that Jesus willingly went through all he did so we could live eternally with him one day. I can't say that I would have willingly endured what I endured for anything or anyone, much less for people who didn't even care about me. But that is what Jesus did. He could have stopped the arrest and execution. He was God incarnate. But he didn't. He allowed it so you and I could live abundantly here on earth and everlastingly after our time here is finished. All he asks of us is that we make him Lord and Savior of our lives and souls. Even in the midst of tragedy, suffering, heartache, and disappointment, we can say we have a hope that does not disappoint, due to the willing submission of Jesus.

Although our faith in things always working out the way we envision may get shattered, and although our positive mental attitude on life may be shaken, we still have the Lord, our Rock and Redeemer. We may not be happy with the way God allows things to go, and we may have a million questions and doubts about life in general. However, no matter what we may face, we still have the hope that Jesus is who he said he is. He is God's Son, the promised Messiah, the Savior. We still have the assurance that due to his work on the cross and his defeat of death through his resurrection, our eternity can be secure by trusting in him.

Because of this, Ryanne and I had the peace of mind that our two little girls were at home in heaven. If Sophia didn't make it, she would be there too. We now understand that even if this life is not fair and bad things do happen to good people, the fact that our Lord became the ultimate sacrifice for us and paid our way into heaven is the only thing that really matters.

If life was grand here on earth, but we had no hope in eternity, what good would all the blessings in the world be? Our time on the sphere of earth is but a breath in the scope of eternity. No matter what our lot here, our salvation is secure, and it will never be changed. We will all go through challenges that make us terribly sad and cause us to question everything, but we can be forever happy in the knowledge of the love of our God. That is his will, perfected.

Sophie Was Fading

On Saturday night, Sophia's body started doing strange things too disturbing to write about. Around 10:30 PM, Pastor DJ came by to talk. He wanted to see how we were holding up emotionally. He seemed to be checking up on Ryanne more than me, and he wanted to know how Ryanne was handling the probability of losing her last baby.

"Not good, of course," I said. "But God has seen Ryanne through thus far; I am sure he will continue."

It was a sad thought that we might soon not have any children. Since October, we had been preparing to be parents. Actually, we had been preparing to be parents our entire lives. Just a few short weeks ago, we *were* parents to three precious girls. Now we were parents to only one. Ryanne's consuming passion had been taking care of our babies, from being there with them all the time, to doing the breast pump religiously (we had an entire deep freezer full of bottles of milk), to waking in the middle of the night to call and check on them, to planning the nursery. If Sophie did not make it, what then? How would we, especially Ryanne, get back to normal life? Her regular life of going to work had ceased weeks ago. It would be hard for her to go back to who she used to be. She was such a different person now. We both were. We both are.

DJ and I talked for nearly an hour. I didn't want to stay away from Ryanne and Sophie that long, but I had some things to talk through. I don't usually open up about my feelings, and I may have been holding a lot of things in for the past several months. It was good for me to talk with DJ and start working things out emotionally.

Ryanne and Sophie had some quality time alone while I was gone. Since I had been there with Ryanne that entire week, they had not had their regular "girl time." When I was working, I would sometimes arrive at the NICU unannounced and find Ryanne singing to Sophia. I loved hearing her sing "Mr. Moon."

"Mr. Moon, moon, bright and silvery moon, hiding behind the tree. Mr. Moon, moon, bright and silvery moon, won't you please shine down on, please shine down on, please shine down on me, me, me, me, me." She would also sing "Jesus Loves Me." I loved walking in on those moments.

Sophia's condition had not changed when I arrived back upstairs after speaking with DJ in the canteen. She was suffering greatly. We wanted her to be healed so badly, but it looked like her death was imminent. Ryanne and I took turns holding her through the night. As the hours wore on, it became more obvious that she was hanging on by a thread. Eternal healing now seemed like the only viable option for our little angel.

We hated to do it, but we felt we needed to sleep for a little while. We told Sophie goodnight and went to lie down for a little nap at about 3:00 AM. I got up an hour later to check on Sophia. She was doing better than she had been all day. Her heart rate and oxygen levels were up. Her heart rate was in the low 100s. I went back and relayed the good news to Ryanne. We had confidence that God was performing a miracle as we slept. We felt like it was Christmas Eve! If we could just fall asleep, when we awoke a wonderful surprise would await us—a recovering Sophia. We slept soundly, believing that God was working mightily in the other room, and we were at peace.

The next time we awoke it was around 8:00 AM on Sunday. I went out to see how well Sophia was doing. The nurse looked directly at me as I walked out the door. Her face was not joyous as I expected but intense and grave. "She's in the 60s," she said. "You'll want to get out here."

I stepped into the transition room and summoned Ryanne. Back at Sophia's bedside, I asked the nurse if anything had happened in the past few hours, because she had been doing so well just a short time ago. The nurse said that nothing drastic had happened. Sophie was just fading.

What torture! A couple of hours ago it seemed as if she was in the middle of a miraculous turnaround, but now she was doing worse than Vivian had been when they started CPR on her. The nurses took Sophie out of the bed so we could hold her. We had our daily time of prayer and Bible reading with her. Ryanne held her, and then it was my turn.

Time passed, and Sophia remained. Her stats increased a little when we got back out there with her. Then they would suddenly drop. Then they would go back up. Then they would drop. The roller coaster continued.

We prayed and prayed and prayed for God to heal her and stop her suffering. We came to the point where we wanted her healing completely and totally, no matter how it came, earthly or heavenly. We just wanted Sophia's pain to end. We wanted her, but we wanted her well more than we wanted her to remain on earth. Ryanne and I began to understand what it meant to be selfless. The Bible teaches us in John 15:13 that "Greater love has no one than this: to lay down one's life for one's friends." We realized we needed to be willing to lay down our lives and desires to raise our little girl so that God could heal her eternally if that was what he chose to do.

The doctor came by and explained that Sophia's recovery was medically impossible, considering how low her heart rate and oxygen saturation were. Her tissues were too damaged from the lack of oxygen. If we wanted to cut off her life support, then it would be understandable and acceptable. If we wanted to help end our baby's misery, then all we had to do was tell them. They reminded us that we would not be ending her life because only God could do that. We would just be agreeing to not prolong her death and suffering.

Stopping the Ventilator

What a horrible decision to be faced with again! With Reece and Vivian, we had to tell the medical team when to stop trying to revive them. That command was difficult enough by itself, but now we had to consider stopping life support altogether. If her body had been physically capable of accepting CPR, then the doctor would have already done that a few days ago. If her heart rate had not jumped back to the low nineties after the CPR, they would have stopped CPR and not hooked her back up to the ventilator. That is what happened with Reece and Vivian. In terms of heart rate and oxygen level, Sophia was already past the point where they started resuscitation on her sisters. Still, Ryanne and I were not ready to make that call just yet.

The day before, one of the RTs and Sophia's nurse had approached us with a suggestion. Considering Sophia's condition, they could arrange for us to take her home in an ambulance, while hooked up to the machines. When we arrived home, we could take her to her room, keep her hooked up to the ventilator for a while, and then stop life support. That way we could at least have the opportunity to take one of our children home. The problem was, that meant Sophia would die at home. We decided against that option. We were not sure she could withstand the trip home, considering her delicate condition. We also didn't want to bring our only baby home just to die. We wanted to leave all the bad memories and images at the NICU … as if they weren't already burned eternally into our minds and hearts.

Our families came up after church that Sunday and sat out in the lobby. They must have sensed that things were not looking good. Ryanne and I went out and told them that Sophia's time was near. It was difficult to relay that message because it was difficult for us to accept that reality. We didn't want to face the fact that our last little girl was about to pass.

When we arrived back at Sophia's bedside we saw that she had taken a turn for the worse. The previous day, she'd begun having seizures. Her little arms and hands would shake, and her hands would lock down into tight fists. The seizures would last for thirty to sixty seconds. Throughout the morning on that Sunday, the seizures increased in intensity and frequency. Other horrors were still occurring with her body. They were worsening, as well, but I will spare the details. She was suffering beyond words; her existence had become pure misery.

I sat down beside Ryanne as she held Sophia close in her arms. We held her together and prayed that God would take care of her and her sisters. We knew she would soon be gone. We prayed that when we gave the command we were about to give, God would sustain Sophia, heal her, and let her live. But we ultimately prayed, "Lord, your will be done."

I stepped outside the curtains that had been pulled around us all day. I told the RT we were ready.

"For what?" she asked, looking and sounding confused.

"To stop the vent," I said.

Although the medical team had suggested it, the nurse and RT appeared shocked that we had actually come to that decision. So were we.

"To stop the vent" became the most difficult phrase I have ever had to say, and the most difficult decision we have ever had to make. Sophia was our last baby, and I had just ordered the nurses to end her life. Dealing with that is more than heart-wrenching.

The doctor, nurse, and RT came behind the curtain with us and asked if we were still okay with what we had requested a few minutes before. Of course we were not okay with it! But it was the right thing to do for Sophia's welfare. Our baby had suffered long enough. If God wanted to heal her and let her live, then when the vent came out, she would breathe and live. If God wanted to take her home to be with him and her sisters, then he would take her. We would succumb to the demands of his plan. We are his, bought at a price, and so was Sophia.

The nurse removed some of Sophia's IVs. The RT turned off the ventilator and took out Sophie's breathing tube. It was nice to see our baby's entire face with no breathing tube taped to it. She was beautiful. She had the most perfect little nose, eyes, and lips—just like her mama. She looked like a chubby little cherub.

We told Sophie we loved her so much and that we would miss her more than she could imagine. We cried ... and we cried ... and we cried. We told little Sophia we loved her and hoped she understood our decision. We didn't want to see her go, but we also didn't want to see her needlessly suffer any longer.

As Ryanne held her, we watched her little chest rise and fall, rise and fall. Then it didn't rise anymore. It was over. Sophia Renee was gone. Her hopeless earthly situation was now eternally hopeful as she went to be with the Lord and her sisters. God's will had been done.

Sophia's Funeral

We held Sophia's funeral two days later. Our music minister, Steve, learned a song we requested him to sing at the service. The song was "Homesick," by Mercy Me. We heard the song for the first time on the radio the morning after Vivian's funeral. The song speaks of losing a loved one and the chorus replies, "I close my eyes and I see your face. If home's where my heart is, then I'm out of place." Those words couldn't have been more appropriate for how Ryanne and I felt now that we were still here on earth and our three precious babies were in heaven. We wanted to be with them so badly.

DJ preached on a passage I had read to Sophia from her little Bible. It was an account of one of Jesus' miracles. In the story, a little girl had died. Jesus went into her room. "He took her by the hand and said to her, 'Talitha koum!' (which means 'Little girl, I say to you, get up!')" (Mark 5:41). And she got up. I envisioned that was what happened on that miserable Sunday when Sophia passed from this life to the

next. Jesus reached out to her and said, "Little girl, get up."
Because of that, neither she nor her sisters will ever be sick
again. They will never suffer any more pain. They will never
have any more heartache.

Her casket was white like her sisters'. She had pink baby
roses on top. We placed her Minnie Mouse and her Bible
on the table beside the casket, told her goodbye, and left
the cemetery.

The girls are buried together, and their marker reads:
*The Lord gave and the Lord hath taken away. Blessed be the
name of the Lord*, Job 1:21.

Chapter 28

On Earth As It Is In Heaven

GOD'S WILL. PERSEVERANCE. Character. Hope. I never thought Ryanne and I would care so much about these things. When we were in the middle of the fire with our girls, we commented regularly that whatever God was trying to do with our lives, we really didn't want him to continue trying to do. We didn't want to learn any lessons. We didn't want to grow spiritually. We only wanted our way. We wanted our babies to be healthy and alive. Now, after going through such life events that made no sense to us logically or spiritually, we long for lessons to pull out of the experience, and we actually rejoice that God counted us worthy to stand such a trial for his sake and glory.

One of the greatest lessons we learned was that no matter what we want, God's plans will prevail. We are fine with that reality because we believe that he really does have our best interests at heart, even when all physical evidence is to the contrary. God loves us, and this is evidenced by his work on the cross. Jesus didn't have to come to earth, and he didn't have to endure dying on a cross for the sins of the world. He could have left things the way they were, but he chose to have compassion on us instead. That compassion turned into eternal life for our girls, and we are certain of this hope for ourselves, as well.

We also came to understand that God's ultimate will is not just for us and our family; it is the same for all of humanity. He desires all to choose him and have an abundant life now and an eternal life to look forward to. Based on the entire course of Scripture, God reaches out to everyone because he wants us to recognize him as Lord. He knows he is king. He does not need our approval or our allegiance, but he wants what is best for our lives. He is our loving heavenly Father, the One who knit us together in our mothers' wombs (Ps. 139:13).

God knows our lives here on earth and our eternal existence will be much more pleasant and meaningful if we submit to his authority and give in to his love. Will we face difficulties? Absolutely. Our story was more than difficult. Will we go through times in our lives when our spirits struggle beyond measure? Yes. Ryanne and I didn't know what to make of God, our relationship with him, or whether he even cared about us. But even though we can't grasp the reasoning behind why God allows us to suffer as he sometimes does, we also can't take hold of his immeasurable love for us. No matter what trial we face here on earth, the fact that God sent Jesus to live with the sole purpose of dying for us makes any temporary pain eternally worthwhile. As Romans 8:18 states, "I consider that our present sufferings are not worth comparing with the glory that will be revealed in us." God made us right with himself by sacrificing his Son. What great love and what great hope for now and the future!

I pray you will never forget that God loves you so much that he sent Jesus to pay your way out of hell and into heaven. Jesus was born of a virgin, lived a blameless life, died a criminal's death, and was buried in a borrowed tomb. He endured all of that so we could have a relationship with him and his Father in eternity. Thankfully, the burial is not where the story ends. After three days, Jesus rose from the dead, came out of the tomb, and appeared to many before ascending into heaven, where he now reigns eternally. If we choose, we can serve a risen King who loves us more than we can ever fathom. He loves us more than any bad thing we have ever done. There is no place where the love of Christ does not reach—from the comfort of the living room to the darkest night in a NICU. God's love desperately searches for us.

Allow God's will to be done in your life. Give your life over to him if you haven't already. Ask Jesus to be your Lord and Savior, and discover the joy, hope, and abundance he will place in your life. If you already are a follower of Christ, don't be content with where you are in your relationship with him. Grow closer. Dig deeper. Love him greater. For that is how God loves you.

Epilogue

AVERY CLAIRE O'Sullivan was born on November 27, 2006. She is our fourth daughter. Her life started a bit rocky. She had difficulty breathing at birth and had to stay in the NICU for twenty-four hours hooked up to oxygen and an IV. But she came around quickly and is growing in stature and sweetness daily. We are so thankful that God saw fit to bless us with another baby girl. She is a miracle and a blessing, just like her sisters were.

In July of 2008, we were blessed with another pregnancy. However, we miscarried one month later in August. Yet in November of 2011, God gave our family Isaac Roman, a strong and strapping little boy. He is such a joy and a delight.

We entrust the care of our little babies, Reece, Vivian, Sophia, and O'Sullivan Baby #5 into the hands of our Lord and Savior Jesus Christ. We know he will take care of them forever, and he will do a better job than we could ever hope to do. But, oh, how we wish we had had the opportunity to try! We eagerly await the day when will hold them again. We submit to the will of our Father, our Creator, and Savior of our little babies and of our souls. We don't fully understand his will, but we trust by faith that it must be for the best, because our God is a loving and merciful God. We love him so much for his grace, mercy, and for giving us the opportunity to be parents of our amazing children.

Little children, Mommy and Daddy love and miss you so much! We wish we could be with you and hold you every day. We will be okay, though, because we know you are in the Master's hands. Have fun in heaven. We can't wait to get there, and then we'll all have fun together as a family. Your sister, Avery and brother, Isaac love you, too.

Lord, your will be done. Amen.

WinePressPublishing
Great Books, Defined.

To order additional copies of this book call:
1-877-421-READ (7323)
or please visit our website at
www.WinePressbooks.com

If you enjoyed this quality custom-published book,
drop by our website for more books and information.

www.winepresspublishing.com
"Your partner in custom publishing."

CPSIA information can be obtained at www.ICGtesting.com
Printed in the USA
LVOW06s0722180813

348301LV00006B/13/P